LOST ROOTS

FAMILY, IDENTITY, AND

LOST ROOTS

FAMILY, IDENTITY, AND ABANDONED ANCESTRY

KARL VON LOEWE

atmosphere press

TABLE OF CONTENTS

To my father, Sigmund von Loewe, who kept secrets that even his two children, both professional historians, could not unravel. He had enormous respect for history, even though his own actions muddied its waters.

PROLOGUE

The worn leather passport case and the 1925 pocket calendar had long nested undisturbed at the bottom of the family strongbox. That box had followed my wife and me across the country from home to home for our entire married life. In early 2002, my cousin Bud Moen contacted me with questions about my mother's side of the family, which he was researching after finding a trove of photos. The questions he asked piqued my curiosity in the contents of the passport case. When I took out the carefully-folded documents, photos, and negatives, I found an unexpected wealth of information. I recalled that somewhere deep in the past, my father had used the surname von Loewe Kiedrowski, but I had never known the significance of that compound family name. For years I

Sigmund's 1922 Polish ID

believed that von Loewe was his mother's birth-name, and Kiedrowski his father's surname. He died in 1958, and I didn't remember ever discussing the surname with him. But among the documents in the passport case and contemporaneous with the German passport was a Polish ID from 1922, with my father's photo, and signed by Zygmund Kiedrowski. A journey began.

I joined and participated in several genealogy listservs and began visits to the family history center of a local Church of the Latter-Day Saints to view microfilm from their vault of genealogy records. I spent Saturday mornings spinning through reel after reel of microfilm. I discovered my father's birth record from 1899, then those of his brothers, Johann (born 1882), August (1890), Anastazy (1892), Władysław (1894) and Klemens (1897) and a sister, Maria (1888). Two other sisters, Valeria (1884) and Dominica (1886), died before the age of three. Their parents were Anton von Kiedrowski

"Grandma and Grandpa von Loewe"

and Marianna von Kiedrowska (nee Skwierawska), whom I knew only in a photograph from about 1938 that was captioned simply "Grandma and Grandpa von Loewe." There was some fluidity in the family surname. I recognized the names of only two brothers – Johann and Klemens. The other siblings were totally unknown to me.

Staring into the dark box of the microfilm reader as images of church records whirred by was a step back into my days as an academic historian, when microfilm reading played a role in my research. Working on my dissertation in the Soviet Union, I had many documents filmed for use in future projects. When I returned to the United States, I had them enlarged and copied onto paper using what was called Copy-Flow Xeroxing. Those compact films became massive continuous rolls of 11" wide paper. Yes, I had a long-time intimate relationship with 35mm microfilm.

Most surprising for me was that records had not been destroyed in the wars and occupations that had plagued

Poland in the twentieth century. Eventually, I found a source of records on CDs for parishes unavailable on film. The Bishop of the Catholic Diocese of Pelplin, Poland, was making records available from his various parishes. Consequently, records were being photographed in color using better equipment than the LDS missionaries had at their disposal. I was able to purchase CDs and view them on my computer at will, a far superior experience to burying my head in a microfilm reader on Saturday mornings.

Identifying individuals and charting family groups from parish records was only the first stage of the project. The cast of characters was growing, but their precise roles in the saga were unclear. My next task was connecting these newly-found people with places and events – and hopefully, with living relatives. My familiarity with the region's history was helpful, but I reached out to genealogists of Europe for more assistance. Distant cousins, helpful amateurs and distinguished scholars alike filled my email inbox with leads and knowledge. Slowly a picture emerged from the thousands of puzzle pieces, but so did some new mysteries. As a child, I had heard little more than whispers about relatives in Poland, whom I understood were Germans somehow accidentally caught behind the Iron Curtain after WWII. But it was no accident, and they were not German – nor even Polish, for that matter.

The Coat of Arms of "SvonL"

My sister and I had been raised in what was considered a German-American home, with just a nod given to our mother's

Norwegian roots. We learned German songs. We earnestly studied German in high school and college. The family coat of arms (assumed to be German) was framed and hung prominently on a living room wall. There were photographic coffee table books of Germany in the house, the most massive of which, *Das Goldene Buch des Deutschen Volkes an der Jahrhundertwende* (The Golden Book of German Culture at the Turn of the Century) spilled over the shelf of any bookcase, even flat on its back. There was never any question, of course. We were at least half-German by ancestry! But quite a different picture seemed to be coming into focus as my research progressed.

As I pieced together my father's immediate family, I was struck by the fact that other than that they were born in West Prussia, I knew little about them beyond their birthdates and immediate ancestors. That was especially troubling for me because their adult lives coincided with two world wars, a fact that – for me, at least – begged further investigation. How were they affected? What roles did they play? Who survived two world wars and multiple foreign occupations? What did my father know, and what did he do about it? My close family was duly impressed with my discovery of my father's family, but seemed satisfied with that alone. Sharing information with family members gave me enjoyment that past historical research had lacked, but as data discovery and entry became routine, enthusiasm waned.

The stunning breakthrough came when I learned that I had a first cousin living in Poland. Czesław, Władysław's older son, had known my grandparents and four of my uncles. Czesław's daughter, Katrina, lived in the United States and emailed me after she was contacted by the organizer of a family reunion in Poland who knew about my research into the family. Katrina told her father about me, and he found a letterhead from my father's jewelry store. In a quick email exchange Katrina and I eagerly confirmed the family ties.

Born in 1930, Czesław had experienced the horrors of World War II as a child, events that, as far as I knew, never affected my family directly, but some of which I could now document and see the connection. With Czesław's recall and the information I gathered from the family reunion participants and website, it had become clear my paternal roots were in the Kashubian community of today's northern Poland. Moreover, my research soon revealed that the family name was adjusted over time by both my father and his brother Johann, to reflect the desired ethnic association – in both those cases German. It was both exciting and surprising to discover in the course of my research that my German roots were really Polish, and then that they weren't even really Polish, but Kashubian. Exciting because my long-dormant research skills had uncovered the facts, but surprising because I had expected that the discovery of Polish roots was the definitive answer to the question of my paternal ancestry. Given our upbringing as German-Americans, even the Polish connection made my sister dubious, not to mention her less-than-enthusiastic attitude toward being Kashubian rather than German. It was not what we had grown up believing all our lives, and there was little reason to change that now.

Over the course of two years, I exchanged information with Czesław through Katrina. This retired electrical engineer had no computer, nor did he want one. Only reluctantly did he have telephone service, chiefly to be able to talk with his daughter. Katrina would call him every Saturday posing any questions I asked her, and he would respond. She would then forward his answers to me via email. On rare occasions he and I would correspond in German via postal mail. We took turns stunning each other. He was surprised by some of my discoveries, and I was amazed by some of his stories. Our convoluted system of information sharing primed the pump for our eventual personal meetings.

A family reunion was scheduled for August 2008, the

eighth in as many years, at an agri-tourism center in the village of Pażęce, Poland. That was the main reason I had persuaded my wife, Judy, sister, Gretchen Kreuter, nephew, David Kreuter, and cousin, Ray von Loewe, and his wife, Barbara, to visit Poland. Remarkable about the family reunion was that it was of a family surname none of us had ever really known prior to my research. As my investigations progressed, first with discovering my father's old passport and learning his birth name – Siegmund Leo v. Kiedrowski – more surprises were discovered, leading me to the "Lew-Kiedrowski" family reunion. But not even that revealing and hugely entertaining occasion would take precedence over conversations with Czesław.

Father's Residence		Father's Name	Mother's Name & Birthname	Date of Birth	Child's Name
Abbau Jezewo	*Jo*	*Anton v. Kiedrow ski*	*Anna geb. Skwierewska*	*2 I 55*	*Siegmund Leo*

Sigmund's 1899 Baptismal Record

We arrived in Gdańsk on August 19, 2008. Early on that Tuesday evening, our hotel restaurant was less than half-full as Judy and I, Gretchen and David, sat around the table for our first meal with Czesław and his wife, Tamara. We were joined by Katrina and her husband, Mark. Barb and Ray arrived after dinner. The occasionally lively and frequently stumbling conversations in Polish, German, English and Russian spilling from our table may have intrigued the other early diners. Czesław and I were first cousins; our fathers were brothers who parted in 1927 as young men. His remained here in Poland, mine settled in America. We had come together to swap my research and his fading photographs of memory. Czesław was appropriately frail for someone who had endured what he had over his lifetime, but his memory was not frail, nor did his clear blue eyes wander. We had met for the first time just a few hours earlier at the airport, after Judy, Gretchen, and I arrived on a flight from Warsaw. David had arrived a bit earlier.

As we walked to dinner, Czesław made clear the linguistic ground rules for the two of us. Because of his lack of English and my virtual lack of conversational Polish, we would converse in German, and we

Czesław (L) and the author

would address each other as "Du", the familiar form of "you" in German. My German left much to be desired. Russian was the foreign language I stumbled least in, but using it with Czesław would have been not only nonproductive, but inappropriate, given Poland's history. The only exception was when I spoke with his wife, Tamara, who spoke Polish and Russian, but no German. That worked to Judy's advantage, as she managed to have some nice conversations with Tamara in Russian. Crucial to any exchange of information was Czesław's daughter, Katrina, who had joined us on this trip, together with Mark, another native of Gdańsk. She and Mark did yeoman's service as everyone's translators.

Over the next several days, Czesław related stories from his life and that of his brother Zbigniew, who had died just two years before. I had viewed thousands of documents in my investigations, but they were flat and impersonal, and unsurprisingly poor conversationalists. Our discussions ranged far and wide, from early family memories to recent politics. Generally shy, Czesław often was animated in his responses to my questions, though sometimes a bit gruff, especially when I raised points with which he took issue, such as my father's insistence on being considered German.

My conversations with Czesław clarified for the first time how World War II affected our family. Every brother in Poland, Anastazy, Klemens and Władysław, was arrested and sent to concentration camps. Anastazy was a prisoner of war executed by the Soviets. Klemens and Władysław were interned in Nazi labor camps. Alone among the siblings, there is no record or recall of Maria being arrested. Władysław's wife had also spent years in a Nazi work camp. Anastazy's wife was arrested and imprisoned briefly for underground activity. Their experiences in the war were easily confirmed now that I knew their names. The early, indistinct pictures from my research now took on a vividness I had never anticipated. Yet there remained the questions of my uncles' families' post-war lives.

Other family members were of great assistance. My cousin, Ray, sent me dozens of letters received by his father, Hans von Loewe, from the family of Sigmund's brother Johann in Germany, letters written from 1937 to 1972 (with a seven-year gap during World War II). I was able to transcribe and translate them for him and his family. The postwar letters starkly revealed the difficult times they endured during the occupation of Germany. Another cousin, Ryszard Felski in Poland, grandson of Anastazy, shared family photos with me as well as a letter my father wrote to Ryszard's mother (Sigmund's niece) in 1946 in response to her plea for help. Sigmund's reply to her was only one of the actions he took as his brothers, sister, nieces and nephews suffered in the aftermath of World War II. Some of his efforts I recalled vaguely from childhood. Others stunned me when I learned of them for the first time from Czesław.

After Ray and Barb left to fly home to the U.S., Judy, Gretchen, David and I left Poland to spend two days in Berlin to decompress from our visit with relatives, new friends and members of the Kashubian community. Especially memorable for our stay in Berlin was when David and I traveled from Berlin to Sachsenhausen concentration camp where Czesław's father, Władysław, was interned for three years. It seemed a fitting, though sad, capstone to our trip, which in one week had uncovered and defined with unexpected clarity our multilayered ethnicity.

———

Between 1923 and 1931, my father and his brother, Johann, formally changed their surnames in order to reflect a more acceptable ethnicity in their countries of choice, falsifying or at least abandoning their ancestry, removing the most obvious indicator of otherness in order to better fit in. Johann's actions were more urgent in light of societal trends in Germany. But for Sigmund, by closeting his Kashubian and Polish roots he easily entered the U.S. in 1923 as a German. He doubled down with a surname change from Kiedrowski to von Loewe on his petition for citizenship in 1930, identifying as a member of what was then (and is still today) the largest ethnic group by origins in America, but at that time also one of the most reviled nationalities on earth as the cause of World War I. As both a family member and a historian, I needed to learn what prompted the assertion of false ancestry and the abandonment of their heritage.

Although the discovery of abandoned ancestral roots was gratifying, meeting cousins in Poland provided knowledge far beyond what I ever expected and taught me much about my immediate family. It was from the Polish family members that I learned the actions Sigmund took following the second world war. There had been no correspondence in seven years. For more than a year after the conclusion of hostilities in Europe, he was unable to get assistance to his family. The measures he took to overcome government barriers bordered on the heroic. His actions, often creative and inspired, were little less than a frantic race against time to find and save survivors from starvation and death.

What had begun as a simple family genealogy project, with its promise of warm feelings of new knowledge about family, chilled me more than once, as I learned of family heroes and war crime victims, and those who went missing in combat, or were trapped behind the Iron Curtain. Initial curiosity led to the recall of the historical context discovered during my graduate student days. Knowing that context raised more questions, and created a deeply personal connection to family. Many times I regretted not asking my father questions that would have revealed important events in his life and that of his family abroad. But he had died when I was a college freshman, and seventeen is not an age for that sort of inquisitiveness. Family genealogists often discover too late that the best sources of information have passed on before they could be interviewed. Would more information from him have changed the direction of research as a professional historian? Most likely, but that is a question for another time. Ultimately, this family tree has deeper roots and broader, gnarlier branches than I ever imagined. And there are mysteries and secrets that remain. That worn passport case had changed my life.

THE DESCENDANTS OF ANTON VON KIEDROWSKI

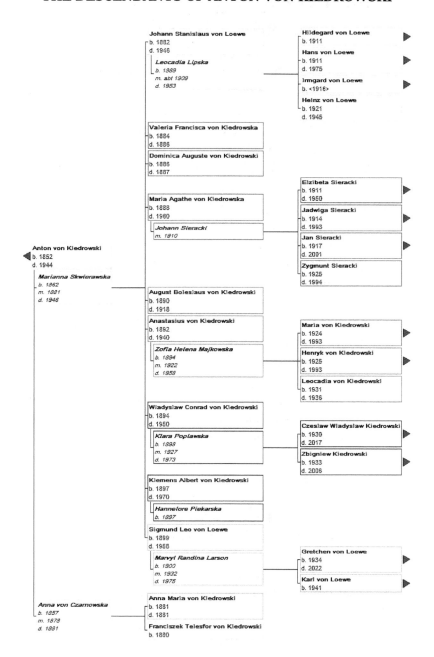

Johann Stanislaus von Loewe
b. 1882
d. 1946
Leocadia Lipska
b. 1889
m. abt 1909
d. 1953

Hildegard von Loewe
b. 1911

Hans von Loewe
b. 1911
d. 1975

Irmgard von Loewe
b. <1916>

Heinz von Loewe
b. 1921
d. 1945

Valeria Francisca von Kiedrowska
b. 1884
d. 1886

Dominica Auguste von Kiedrowski
b. 1886
d. 1887

Maria Agathe von Kiedrowska
b. 1888
d. 1980
Johann Sieracki
m. 1910

Elzibeta Sieracki
b. 1911
d. 1950

Jadwiga Sieracki
b. 1914
d. 1993

Jan Sieracki
b. 1917
d. 2001

Zygmunt Sieracki
b. 1925
d. 1994

Anton von Kiedrowski
b. 1852
d. 1944
Marianna Skwierawska
b. 1862
m. 1881
d. 1946

August Boleslaus von Kiedrowski
b. 1890
d. 1918

Anastasius von Kiedrowski
b. 1892
d. 1940
Zofia Helena Majkowska
b. 1894
m. 1922
d. 1958

Maria von Kiedrowski
b. 1924
d. 1993

Henryk von Kiedrowski
b. 1925
d. 1993

Leocadia von Kiedrowski
b. 1931
d. 1936

Wladyslaw Conrad von Kiedrowski
b. 1894
d. 1950
Klara Poplawska
b. 1899
m. 1927
d. 1973

Czeslaw Wladyslaw Kiedrowski
b. 1930
d. 2017

Zbigniew Kiedrowski
b. 1933
d. 2006

Klemens Albert von Kiedrowski
b. 1897
d. 1970
Hannelore Piekarska
b. 1897

Sigmund Leo von Loewe
b. 1899
d. 1968
Marvyl Randina Larson
b. 1900
m. 1932
d. 1975

Gretchen von Loewe
b. 1934
d. 2022

Karl von Loewe
b. 1941

Anna von Czarnowska
b. 1857
m. 1878
d. 1881

Anna Maria von Kiedrowski
b. 1881
d. 1881

Franciszek Telesfor von Kiedrowski
b. 1880

CHAPTER ONE
The Watchmaker's Apprentice

It was no place like home. Three months after his fourteenth birthday, Sigmund von Kiedrowski was in the village of Putzig, Germany. It was April 1913, and he was far away from home. Far away from family, including his six siblings, all older than him. Far away from the village he was born in. Far away from the rolling hills, lakes and small farms. This community was not only smaller, but seaside. On the northwest shore of the eponymous bay, really more of a lagoon connected to the Baltic Sea, this was a village of about two thousand people. For more than a millennium, it had been a modest seaport and marketplace, and for all those centuries, commercial fishing and boating were common occupations.

This unfamiliar, even alien town was where he would serve his apprenticeship in watchmaking with the master Franz Golembiewski. Since medieval times it had been common for apprentices to live with the master's family; so it was with Sigmund during his three years of apprenticeship at Franz's side. Franz and Maria Golembiewski[1] had jewelry and watchmaking stores in both Danzig (now Gdańsk, Poland) and Putzig (now Puck, Poland). Maria ran their retail store, where they sold watches, gold and silver jewelry, violins, flutes, clarinets, all manner of optical goods, and weather instruments.

Sigmund's parents, Anton and Anna von Kiedrowski, were shopkeepers, merchants doing well by the time their youngest was a teen. Learning a trade that could be combined with

---

[1] Throughout this work I will Anglicize the masculine endings of Polish surnames for women, as well as for men, e.g. – Golembiewski (masculine) instead of Golembiewska (feminine). And I will use the English plural Kiedrowskis rather than the normal Polish Kiedrowscy.

general retail shopkeeping seemed a natural choice. Sending him off to a town 100 km away, beyond the influence of his four older brothers who still remained somewhat local, also had much to recommend it. A small coastal village promised fewer distractions for a teenager. Putzig was not as alien culturally as the urban, industrial Essen, Germany, where his oldest brother Johann had settled. But perhaps a central element to his parents' decision was Putzig's ethnic makeup, which coincided with theirs. Though half the size of Berent's, Putzig's population, like Berent, was predominantly Kashubian, and had been for centuries.

———

The ancestral home of the Kashubs is Pomerania, an area along the south coast of the Baltic Sea west from the mouth of the Vistula River to the mouth of the Oder River. For Pomerania not one of those three clearly defined borders is much of an impediment to determined invaders. Pomerania occupies the northern edge of a main path of invasion. In ancient times tribes of barbarians passed through from the east as conquerors of the lands south of the Baltic coast inhabited by the indigenous Slavic tribes, including Polabians, Wends and Kashubs. By the tenth century AD, most of these early tribes had been absorbed, some exterminated, while others had pushed on to greener fields. Of all the Slavic tribes in Pomerania, only the Kashubs survived culturally intact to any degree. Native to the area for centuries, the Kashubs became Christianized in the eleventh and twelfth centuries.

By the thirteenth century, the Kashubs had spread beyond the Oder River into the territory of Germanic tribes. Aggressive Germanization of Slavs that took place along the Baltic coast seems to have been resisted quite successfully by the Kashubs. The resistance was passive; many just moved eastward, away from German influence. Those that stayed behind survived as part of the surrounding German culture, even adopting Protestantism after the Reformation and becoming Germanized. The Kashubs who lived among the Poles shared their Roman Catholic faith, but the Kashubs embraced a nature-based mysticism and a mythology that is not as evident in Polish Catholicism. Their language is often referred to as Old Pomeranian, or just Pomeranian. Some linguists consider it a dialect of Polish. Like Polish, it is one of the five lechitic languages (Polish, Kashubian, Silesian, and the extinct Slovincian and Polabian) of the West Slavic group, but distinct, containing several dialects within it – some not always intelligible to speakers of others.

The Kashubian world underwent profound change following the 1772-1795 Partitions of Poland, a breakup that persisted until 1918. Kashubian nobles sought to secure their landowning monopoly by swearing allegiance to the new sovereign, Frederick the Great, King of Prussia,[2] only to have later agrarian reforms turn holdings of the local Kashubian nobility over to non-nobles.

While in western Pomerania, German domination carried with it Protestantism, the Kashubs' community of faith with Poles to the east and south made it possible for them to survive with many of their cultural institutions intact in spite of significant reshaping of social and economic realities. Kashubian ethnicity existed relatively peacefully side-by-side with Polish, leading to the old saying in Kashubian – "Without Kashubia there is no Poland, without Poland there is no Kashubia."[3] Kashubs claim to have a population as high as five

---

[2] Descendants of these Kashubian nobles now living abroad even today like to claim German ethnicity, much like a cat born in a garage claims to be a car.

[3] From the epic poem, "O Panu Czorlińscim co do Pucka po seces jachoł" ("Mr. Czorlinski goes to Puck to Buy Fishing Nets") by nineteenth century

hundred thousand in today's Poland, and as many as three hundred thousand speak Kashubian on a daily basis. During the period of the Partitions, German was the official language of West Prussia. All public records of the nineteenth century were maintained in German.

From early in the nineteenth century, there was a growing crisis among the Kashubians that would affect them on several fronts. Following the final partition, all of Kashubia was under the control of staunchly protestant Prussia. Anti-Catholic pressure only worsened as the century wore on, and there would be a battle of cultures in the future unified German Empire.

The exclusivity of landowning by Kashubian nobles was ended in 1807. This was a deep social change for a largely agrarian society, but in exchange for this loss, they were offered the opportunity to open businesses in towns and cities in Prussia, becoming part of a growing urban middle class. The almost exclusively rural Kashubs had already found themselves in a worsening economic position, as farms were becoming smaller and smaller as large families divided properties to provide for their heirs. The holdings of many Kashubian families had become too small and of too poor quality from which to make a living, and scores sold out to wealthier (often German) landowners who could assemble small parcels into larger estates.

The increasing industrialization of Europe, especially the German states, offered employment for impoverished, landless agricultural workers. Working in factories in industrialized areas was one of the few options left to them. But by the middle of the nineteenth century, a different kind of opportunity opened up for those who wished to remain small non-owner farmers. At mid-century these potential immi-

---

Kashubian poet Heronim Derdowski. Born in Kashubia, he immigrated to the U.S. after 1885, settling in Winona, Minnesota.

grants were offered free passage to North America and the promise of land, leading to the Kashubian diaspora. Shipping companies, in particular, were eager to develop emigration – after 1860 no longer free – to fill ships that in earlier years were sent empty to North America to bring lumber back to Europe. Increasingly impoverished farmers succumbed to the siren song of promised large tracts of free land in Canada and America, even New Zealand, as an option to emigrating to more urban areas within the Prussian empire. In order to maintain their agrarian way of life, they opted to move to a new country with unfamiliar language and customs. Anton and Anna were among those who stayed behind, choosing to remain within the boundaries of their traditional culture, but pursuing an occupation unfamiliar to their noble, landowning ancestors. Notwithstanding the familiarity of culture, their journey to the future would be difficult and marked by tragedy and sorrow.

———

On April 16, 1881, the Saturday before Easter, Anton von Kiedrowski entered the district clerk's office in the village of Gross Tuchen (now Tuchomie) to report for the civil record the most joyous and the most devastating experiences of his life. For the twenty-eight-year-old Kashubian landowner joyous was the recording of the April 10 birth of his daughter Anna Maria, born to him and his wife of two and one-half years, Anna von Czarnowski. Devastating was the recording of the death of his wife just five days after the birth. She was twenty-three when she died on Good Friday. His shaking hand produced a signature very different from the strong one made on their marriage registration in 1878. The Kiedrowski and Czarnowski families were of deep Kashubian roots, going back many generations of nobility into the sixteenth century and beyond.

The office where Anton recorded his wife's death and daughter's birth was one of the many offices in Prussia that maintained the secular milestones of life. In August of 1881, just four months later, he would again be in that office, signing off on the death of his daughter, age four months and eleven days. With no joy to soften the sorrow, the depth of his grief was profound, revealed by the almost child-like scribble "A.v. Kiedrowski". On September 26 of 1881, widowed and again childless at the age of twenty-nine, Anton remarried, just five months after his wife's death, this time to Marianna Skwierawski. It was not unusual for men his age at that time to remarry quickly, not only in West Prussia, a province of the newly-created Second German Empire, but in other predominantly agrarian societies as well – including the United States. Three daughters, Valeria Francisca (born 1884), Dominica Auguste (1886), and Maria Agathe (1888), and a son, Johann Stanislaus (1882), were born to them in Klein Platenheim (now called Płotowo), a small village of a few hundred farmers not far from Anton's ancestral roots. Eight years later, when their second son, August Boleslaus was born in 1890, the family was living nearly 50 km to the east, across rolling glacial moraines, in the village of Berent Abbau (now called Kościerzyna-Wybudowanie), West Prussia.

For Anton and Anna both, the move to Berent caused sadness, for in addition to the graves of Anton's first wife and daughter, they left behind the graves of two daughters. Both Valeria and Dominica had died before the age of three, but Maria Agathe survived to make the move to Berent. Neither parent was originally from Berent. Anton had been born in 1852 in Czarnowo, south southwest of Berent, the youngest of six siblings. Marianna, better known as Anna, born in 1862, was from Raduhn (now called Radom), also not far from Berent. For Anna, it was a move closer to family roots in that area. Both families had long histories as noble landowners. For them both and their family, it was a move to a less rural environment at a time when their culture was under assault. They left behind a stunning bucolic landscape of lakes and hills, sometimes referred to as the Switzerland of Kashubia. Unlike Klein Platenheim, Berent was a growing town of some four thousand souls that could support trades, crafts and commerce.

Despite the emigration of many Kashubian families like theirs from the area, for Anton and Anna Berent, this represented economic opportunity, especially after the railroad came to the town about 1885. Though just a spur on the main line between Berlin and Königsberg, East Prussia, as well as to Danzig, through it goods moved back and forth across the borders of the German Empire. The railroad was a double-edged sword, for it also connected departing Kashubians with the ports of Hamburg and Bremen, points of embarkation for emigrants leaving their homeland.

The chance to own a general merchandise store in a town on a rail line was attractive enough for Anton to move his small, young family from a place of grief. Shopkeeping may have shown more promise than scratching out a living from the land. Through the custom of the time Anna's dowry made the purchase of, or succession to a store a reality. Just as any "peasant or citizen", not just nobles, could now own landed property, conversely, nobles could now engage in "city occupations", allowing land-poor Kashubian nobles to become owners of commercial and industrial enterprises – if they had the capital. Anton realized his future in this growing class of shopkeepers, though as a Kashubian, he was caught in an economic and cultural struggle between Poles and Germans.

Anton's roots in Kashubian nobility can be documented from at least the early seventeenth century, when the family had adopted the Lew coat of arms. In the Polish manner of the time, other noble families completely unrelated to the Kiedrowskis also used that coat of arms. They were landowners, but like many Kashubian families noted above, large generation after large generation led to smaller and smaller plots of land, until there wasn't much in the way of fertile land left to till or raise livestock. Anton had five brothers and one sister. His eldest brother was twenty years his senior. His future would lie in commerce, making it possible for his children to adapt and thrive in their changing world. But that imperative could be hindered by two factors: aggressive German cultural colonialism and the family's Catholicism, rocky shoals between which he and his family – along with other Kashubs and Poles as well – had to navigate carefully.

Kashubs and Poles had in common their Catholic faith, and after 1871 they were citizens of the German Empire. There were many families that spoke Polish or even Kashubian – the Kiedrowski family was one of those that spoke Kashubian at home. German, however, was the language of schools and government – and inevitably, personal advancement. Polish was spoken in church and read in newspapers. But Anton and Anna's children were born into something other than simply a German Catholic world. All the siblings were born in the last two decades of the nineteenth century, when virulent nationalism became a prelude to the savage twentieth century

Germanization had only in-tensified by the time Sigmund was born, but Sigmund and his siblings were born into a Catholic world. With the ex-ception of Johann and Maria, who were born in Klein Platen-heim, their baptisms were in the Holy Trinity Church of Berent, unusual for typical citizens of the German world. Most ethnic Germans in Pomerania were Evangelical (Protestant), not

Sigmund's First Communion

Roman Catholic. But Sigmund's life was a Catholic one, including his First Communion. A photo of him, ramrod-straight, dressed in a suit and white bow tie, holding a cross in his right hand and prayer book in his left, testifies clearly to his formal spiritual affiliation at that time.

The children of Anton and Anna were born into a home that was Kashubian, a world that they knew as German and Catholic, but a world that only later would they learn was unexpectedly turbulent and brutal, affecting them on a profoundly personal scale.

Little is known about the siblings' childhoods. We do know that at some point in Sigmund's childhood, he contracted rheumatic fever, usually caused by a streptococcus infection. It was rheumatic fever complicated by asthma that damaged his heart, and led to his death at a relatively young age. Closest in age to Sigmund was Klemens, just two years older. Klemens and Sigmund would become the closest of the brothers, not just in age but in personality as well, both with a dry wit and a talent for business success.

The eldest of the surviving siblings was Johann Stanislaus, born in 1882. Born seventeen years before Sigmund, and despite the wide gap in ages and resultant absence, Sigmund and Klemens were deeply influenced by their big brother Johann, even though he left home before they were in their teens. He was the family pioneer, leaving the home in West Prussia and establishing himself in the more industrialized western region of the German Empire, in the heartland of Germany's heavy industry, the Ruhr Valley. Johann had made his move to the Rhine Province – specifically, the city of Essen – by 1911, joining others attracted to the Krupp armament industry and other coal and steel enterprises. By the time he settled in Essen, its population had swelled to over one hundred thousand.

What little we know about Johann before 1937 reveals someone who saw himself as German, not Polish or Kashubian. Johann left West Prussia and settled in Essen with his wife, Leocadia Lipski, a woman born in Lipa, about 20 km south of Berent. He took on the more familiar, Germanized form of his given name – Hans. He and his wife were married in Essen, about 1909. As late as 1912, Hans was still using the Kiedrowski surname, but after that year, it slipped away, and Johann went by the name Hans von Loewe which he formalized in 1931.[4] They would raise their four children in Essen during the very troubled times ahead.

As Germany strove to be competitive in industrializing Europe, public education became a crucial element in the campaign. Not only did workers have to acquire skills necessary for the shop floor, but citizens had to learn management skills as well. Management proficiency was required to sustain the existence and profitability of the new corporate organizations, and Johann had sufficient education to allow him to avoid the shop floor. An expansive tram system had been created in 1894 to connect urban neighborhoods and surrounding villages with Essen's shops, mills, and factories. After a few short years working elsewhere, he found employment with the burgeoning Essen public transit system. Managed for Essen by South German Railway Company (Süddeutsche Eisenbahngesellschaft – SEG), in 1911, SEG and the city of Essen signed an agreement that would lead to an explosive expansion of the system in the same year as Johann joined it. He was a bookkeeper, accountant and finance specialist. He worked there until his death nearly thirty-five years later. But that apparently admirable unwavering career path was eclipsed by what was a much more complicated personal life and a role in his brothers' lives that stirs controversy to this day.

---

[4] See Chapter Six, "Johann, His Family, and His Agenda," for the unusual specifics of this change.

—

As the last to leave the family home, Sigmund, sent away from home at the age of fourteen, traveled north, not west. For the short term, at least, his parents made certain that his further education would not only be practical, but safely within the Kashubian cultural sphere. By that time, his siblings were already preparing for or working at what they saw as their careers, but any intention they had to follow in Johann's footsteps would be delayed.

For their youngest son's apprenticeship, his parents had chosen a quiet location in a small seaside village in an area largely populated by fellow Kashubs. It seemed ideal. But three months after their son's arrival, airplanes unexpectedly became a regular distraction, as the Imperial German Navy established its naval air arm headquarters and seaplane base in Putzig. The establishment of the air base and the effect it would have on their son likely never entered into their calculations.

The awkwardly delicate machines flew in low and loud, overwhelming the most obnoxious seagulls, being far bigger and more deafening. Jinking in the wind, they landed with a resounding slap on the water, churning toward the shore with only slightly less racket, chasing the gulls from what had been their private Putzig beach. In that time of increasing public fascination with flying, no small-town fourteen-year-old could ignore them – indeed, could not help being enchanted by them. And Sigmund would have been no exception. The care with which Anna and Anton had selected a locale for Sigmund's education beyond the six years of *Realschule* was in vain.

Gangly multi-engine flying boats with bulbous hulls and other, more delicate single-engine floatplanes with giant pontoons dangling beneath them became a common site. A grass runway led to a boat ramp with a crane that was used to hoist planes in and out of the water as needed. Much of the activity disappeared a year later when the headquarters of the naval arm was moved. Reduced flights continued, especially when war broke out, and the base became the primary seaplane station for the Baltic. But even the less frequent coming and going of aircraft could not be missed by this young teenager, away from home for the first time in a totally new learning and life environment.

Sigmund did not spend all his time hunched over a workbench or transfixed by lumbering seaplanes. He sailed a bit, enjoying it even when it led to an unintended dunking, recalled decades later. But from the time he arrived in 1913, he spent the next six years either peering through an eye loupe at escapements, pins and pivots, or wedged in the cockpit of one of those preternaturally noisy contraptions – and he preserved documents connected with both activities until the day he died. They were an essential part of who he was.

When war broke out in August 1914, Sigmund was already engrossed in the table-top machine shop that could create the fine tolerances constituting watchmaking and repair. He was away from home to learn a trade and serve his apprenticeship. After completing his apprenticeship with Golembiewski, he began his professional life with a glowing letter of reference, then went on to pass the certification process from the board of examiners in Danzig. In his letter of reference on April 1, 1916, Golembiewski wrote:

> "I hereby certify that the watchmaker helper Sigismund von Kiedrowski of Berent, from April 1, 1913 to April 1, 1916 has had the benefit of watchmaking study with me. Through eager diligence he has at the same time acquired the necessary and possible knowledge as well as thoroughly prepared for his future career. His good character is a further good point. I recommend him most warmly to my colleagues and I wish him to be one day a diligent worker."

On July 6, 1916, the West Prussian handicraft guild in Danzig certified him as a journeyman in watch repair, noting that "Sigismund v. Kiedrowski" was from Putzig, West Prussia, his residence for the past three years. Much like the classic journeymen of medieval Europe, Sigmund could now work for a master and be paid on a daily basis, moving around the country (and ultimately

Journeyman's Certificate

abroad), holding a series of "watchmaker helper" (German: *Uhrmacherhilfer*) jobs for the next ten years. As proof of his status, he carried his certificate with him to every new job. As he collected a letter of reference, he would fold it neatly and keep it with others – many of them contained in his passport case until his death more than forty years later.

After completing his apprenticeship with Franz on April 1, 1916, Sigmund's first journeyman job was working for Maria in the Golembiewskis' store in Putzig. He worked for her until March 1, 1917, when he left. According to Maria's letter of reference, it was at Sigmund's request that she released him from employment in the shop.

With the exception of the naval air station, Putzig was distant from the action in World War I, so when Sigmund left his first place of employment, he became exposed personally for the first time to the turmoil that had been going on since the second year of his apprenticeship. He was probably not leaving the Golembiewskis as voluntarily as it may have seemed. A war was on, and he was called to serve.

His childhood within the familiar Kashubian community

had come to an end. The harsh reality of life outside now intervened with its hurdles, snares and pitfalls, a seventy-five-year period of war, revolution and repression, during which tens of millions of soldiers and civilians would be killed or disappear, and tens of millions more displaced. Only Sigmund, of all his siblings, would escape the physical brutality of that age, which for his brothers and sister would include wartime capture or disappearance, concentration camp internment, starvation, political execution, or violent repression, but his wounds, though not physical, would be deep, permanent – and hidden.

CHAPTER TWO
Warbird

After a year of casualties and unexpectedly extended conflict, by 1916, early enthusiasm for enlisting flagged in Germany, and the calls for soldiers went out earlier and earlier as the need increased. Those who under peacetime conditions would have reported in 1918 were called up in two classes, September 1916 and January 1917. Sigmund's twentieth birthday would occur in 1919, but men of that class year were called up in January and February or May and June of 1917. Even under the pre-war criteria, four of Sigmund's brothers would have been subject to conscription: August in 1910, Anastazy in 1912, Władysław in 1914 and Klemens in 1917, and so it would have come as no surprise to him. Johann, aged thirty-two and father of two children when the war broke out, would have done his service starting in 1902, and by the time of the outbreak of war was most likely serving in the reserves, the *Landsturm,* for which he was liable until the age of 45.[5]

Released from his job on March 1 by Maria Golembiewski, Sigmund was free to report to the military for his physical. The urgent need for new troops led to the accelerated and expedited integration of new draftees. Basic training took place early and quickly, but the specifics of his service from March of 1917 to when he was mustered out of military air service on April 15, 1919, at the Graudenz (now Grudziądz) airfield are undocumented. Since that was the base from which he was discharged, it is plausible that Graudenz was where he reported initially. There were at least a dozen different air units moving through Graudenz in the turmoil of

---

[5] R.H. Keller, "The German Soldier in World War I: The Final 'Argument of Kings'," (2009), accessed October 15, 2020, https://greatwar.com/the-german-soldier/.

demobilization in 1918 and 1919. Graudenz was relatively local to his birthplace, and the German army sought to keep locals together when inducted into military units.

Those in Sigmund's call-up were put to duty in the military by April, a pivotal month in the war for two reasons. The first was that on April 6, 1917, the United States entered the war. The Central Powers were not surprised, but the entry caused some significant changes in Germany's prosecution of the war. April was also the famous "Bloody April", during which the Royal Flying Corps suffered staggering casualties at the hands of the German air forces. The ratio of planes lost favored the Germans four to one. It was, however, the last time the German air service held the winning hand, as their short-lived advantage of having the only aircraft with synchronized machine guns disappeared. British and French planes soon reversed their fortunes with new aircraft and better weaponry. A month of great triumph in the air quickly turned into a downward spiral.

Of the technologies introduced during the First World War, among them machine guns and tanks, none more changed the conduct of that and future conflicts than the airplane. It was the airplane that brought a new spatial dimension to warfare. The back-and-forth shuffling of infantry in mass charges, or simply the hunkering down of soldiers in trenches, was now threatened from above.

For the civilian public, air warfare became a romantic respite from the gruesome static reality of trench warfare. In fact, even in the first decade of the century, the public had been enchanted by aviation, as airships like the zeppelin had incredible followings in Germany.[6] The "air-mindedness" of the German populace made it natural for pilots to become

---

[6] Peter Fritzsche, *A Nation of Fliers: German Aviation and the Popular Imagination.* (Cambridge, MA: Harvard University Press, 1992), p.9 and *passim.*

extraordinary propaganda tools in war. Publishing houses that in the past had printed and sold postcard photos of royalty, now switched to producing postcards of aviators such as Oswald Boelcke, Max Immelmann and Manfred von Richthofen ("The Red Baron" as he came to be called after his death). With every promotion or award, cards were re-issued for the biggest names, such as von Richthofen. Probably the most likely citation to warrant a postcard tribute was the Pour le Mérite, or "Blue Max", the most prestigious combat award. Even the funerals of these rock-stars of World War I were photographed and published as postcards. Yet most pilots were anonymous until they had their fifth victory and were termed aces.

In the past, it had been the cavalry members who were the objects of excitement and attention of the civilian population. Cavalrymen were dashing aristocrats for the most part. But the cavalry was fading away from a combat role. Now it was the aviators who were exciting and dashing. Appropriately, many of the leading flyers came from the ranks of the cavalry, such as von Richthofen, and were members of the aristocracy. Like the cavalry, however, flying in 1914 was largely a reconnaissance endeavor, with an officer observer and enlisted man pilot. In time those airmen of aristocratic origin were outnumbered by the typical sons of the middle class.[7] The majority of the air aces were products of technical schools. They loved the sounds and smells of internal combustion engines, whether aircraft or motorcycles. Less than ten percent of the air aces were from the aristocracy. Many successful airmen were accustomed to working with their hands, greasy with the fluids of their interests. They were technicians with a knowledge of math and engineering and a passion for flying.

---

[7] David C. Cooke, *Sky Battle: 1914-1918: The Story of Aviation in World War I.* (New York, W.W. Norton, 1970), pp. 282-286, cited in Fritzsche, p. 98.

Young men who prided themselves on their invincibility were easily seduced by flying. It was risky, it was active. It did not involve months sitting in water-logged trenches shooting rats. They were truly in charge of their fate. But it is hard to imagine what was so appealing about sitting behind an unmuffled aircraft engine with its mind-numbing noise and flesh-freezing wind mixed with occasional sprays of various noxious engine fluids assaulting the pilot. Having an observer on board contributed little to the experience, since communication was rarely verbal (possible only when the engine quit), usually consisting of hand signals. Although winter combat in the air was rare, when it did take place, the insulated winter flight suits made the wearers look like they had been inflated, and their faces were slathered with grease to protect them from freezing. Even in summer, when flying at what would be considered slow speeds (under 100 mph generally) at 5000-10,000 feet, it could be cold in an open cockpit. Yet, flyers on both sides experienced huge popularity, especially with members of the opposite sex, a fact which went far to mitigate less-desirable aspects of their service, perhaps duly noted by Sigmund.

A few months before Sigmund entered military service and enrolled in pilot training, the German air service had undergone a major reorganization in response to failures in the first two years. What had been known as the *Flieger-truppen* (air troops) in 1916 became called the *Luftstreits-kräfte* (air force). Innovative tactics and strategies were introduced by the new commander, Ernst von Höppner. New units that would have specific purposes and would be trained and organized accordingly replaced failing multi-taskers. Ground attack squadrons (*Schlachtstaffeln* or Schlastas*)* were created from the old escort squadrons (*Schutzstaffeln* or Schustas*)* and became infantry support. Hunter squadrons (*Jagdstaffeln* or Jastas) were created that summer to take the combat initiative in the air, to destroy enemy observers and bombers over Germany, becoming more aggressive than the old air troops had been.

The entry of America into the war, long-expected but no less a blow, forced Germany to change tactics as well as strategy. One element of this policy was the "America Program". It was decided that the number of air units, most notably the Jastas, had to be doubled in order to counteract the American forces. This put enormous pressure on the training facilities at the various air bases. And it led to highly compressed training in order to meet the expansion goal of five hundred pilots and four thousand support staff just for the Jastas.

By the time Sigmund left the Golembiewskis in March of 1917, the accelerated draft was the new norm. New recruits experienced basic training in a regional army center for the shortened period of no more than three months, and then moved to the front or other facilities for supplemental and more intensive training.

Once trained in the basics of military service as prescribed by the army, with stamina now increased to a level the watchmaker's workbench never required, Sigmund was enrolled as a pilot. Although earlier pilot training had been understandably basic for such a new technology, revised training guidelines, based on types of aircraft and mission changed that even as the process was shortened. Not much in the way of instrument training was required, since initially the cockpit instruments were rudimentary – altimeter and speedometer. Early in the war, compasses were a personal luxury item and usually carried in the pilot's pocket, but eventually they found their way into the cockpit, as did tachometers and engine temperature gauges. Controlling the aircraft, whether on the ground or in the air, tested any pilot's abilities – physical or mental – and many died in undistinguished ways. Life expectancy for new pilots in combat was measured in days, not months.

While Germany was doubling the number of air units and therefore pilots, Sigmund was undergoing his basic training, followed by flight training probably at FEA 8 (*Flieger Ersatz Abteilung* – Flyer Replacement Unit) in Graudenz. Surviving documents confirm that Sigmund was a pilot. Beyond that, however, not much is known. Once out of the flight training classroom, aspiring pilots like Sigmund had to complete hands-on assignments, including five landings on airfields unknown to the candidate, landing within 50 meters of a fixed marker. In addition, several cross-country flights of 100 and 250 km each with intermediate landings at unfamiliar airfields, each completed between sunrise and sundown, were required of the pilot trainee. With the creation of the fighter units those pilots-to-be also had to take part in simulated air combat with another aircraft.

Although the requirements for those who would fly unarmed observation planes were different from those for pilots who aspired to ground attack, bombing or fighter squadrons, the examinations were somewhat similar, with at least two things in common. One was that all pilots had to perform multiple dead-stick (unpowered glide) landings, a requirement that did not speak well for the reliability of contemporary aircraft engines. The other was that a student could not become a pilot (German: *Flugzeugführer*) until he had flown over enemy territory ("*über den Feind*"). That second requirement set German pilots apart from their enemy counterparts, who simply completed their flight training and got their "wings". The German pilot badge and the title of pilot represented experience Allied pilots lacked when they first took to the air for combat.

With basic army training now as little as three months, plus a few weeks often just behind the lines, replacement/reinforcement troops could be easily pressed into needed spots, or left in place for further training by non-commissioned officers or officers recovering from wounds before they were rotated back to the front. Flight training by this late in the war took an additional two to three months, although it had been as much as ten months earlier in the war. It was likely that Sigmund's training from raw recruit to full-fledged pilot was no more than six months, placing him in the cockpit by the fall of 1917.

Sigmund was most likely assigned to a ground attack Schlasta unit. Unlike the Jastas, which were largely single-seaters flown by commissioned officers, the Schlasta units were piloted by non-commissioned officers like Sigmund, a carryover from the early days of two-seater observer aircraft, when the pilot was a non-commissioned officer or enlisted man and the observer was an officer. There were not many postcards published about these pilots who rarely were aces, but they were heroes to the infantry who could see immediate results when they would fly in close to the ground, and enemy troops would dive for cover.

Whatever role Sigmund performed in the German air force, its importance to him personally should not be under-estimated. He retained crucial paperwork that documented service, just as he did with proof of his achievement in his profession as a watchmaker and jeweler. He regarded his military flying experience as no less significant to his personal future than his apprenticeship and civilian references. In fact, in addition to discharge papers and recommendations, he preserved an Iron Cross Second Class (*EKII* in German), which suggests he may have experienced some success.

Traditionally, the EKII – two million were awarded to service members in all – has been viewed as an award usually made for a pilot's first kill. One known notable exception was Max Immelmann, who was awarded the EKII after being shot down by a French pilot, but preserving his aircraft by landing behind German lines.[8] Ernst Udet, the greatest German ace to survive the war, had a similar situation, winning the EKII early in his career as a non-commissioned officer pilot after his plane suffered structural failure and he and his officer observer managed to manually hold the plane together until they made it behind German lines.[9]

Sigmund never discussed his military service with friends or family members. Even with Bud Moen, his wife's nephew and an aspiring pilot in the 1930s, he was guarded about his flying. He never mentioned combat. He did recount a story about getting lost in clouds and nearly running out of fuel, but making it back to base safely, perhaps on one of his cross-country qualifying flights. For pilots of the time, this was a common theme for flight in its first three decades. Encountering fog or mist was the real terror of the skies when instruments were few and of little use in the dark. Flying blind was a frequent fear of the early pilots. Jim Larson, another of Sigmund's wife's nephews and an eventual pilot, also heard only that his favorite uncle was "on the other side". No further information was provided.

Sigmund's apparent reticence to discuss his service when he got to America may have had a basis in his sensitivity to fighting on the other side, especially before his naturalization in 1931. Moreover, like many combat veterans in conflicts then and even to this day, Sigmund may have been reluctant to discuss his moments of terror and triumph with someone who had not actively served in the war. There was a shared experience that only combat veterans understood and often carried to their graves even decades later without sharing with non-veterans or even spouses. Watching comrades die and

---

[8] G. VanWyngarden, *Early German Aces of World War I*. (Oxford, England, Osprey Publishing, 2006), p. 13.

[9] Stephen Sherman, "Ernst Udet – Second Highest German Ace of WWI", accessed October 15, 2020, http://www.acepilots.com/wwi/ger_udet.html.

killing enemy counterparts leave deep scars on the human psyche. These days those scars are referred to as post-traumatic-stress-disorder (PTSD). In World War I, they were often referred to as shell-shock. For airmen that combat stress was called aeroneurosis, and pilots' letters published after the war reveal a great deal of psychological suffering.[10]

Bud related that Sigmund seemed to be more interested in the rapid changes in instrumentation than anything else, changes that made it easier to overcome mist and fog. They came rapidly in the late 1920s, in large measure through the efforts of WWI pilots like Jimmy Doolittle of the U.S. The new instruments were now of a precision comparable to watches, instead of the crude gauges like the altimeter that measured height above sea level, not actual altitude above the ground – not terribly useful in limited visibility over high terrains. Of course, by the time they talked, mechanical precision was now Sigmund's profession – instruments that measured time. They were politically neutral and universal. With few exceptions, he simply did not talk about combat flying or even flying in general. It is ironic that something so important to him that he carried to his grave, papers to prove his achievement, should have been the subject of only a few cryptic comments to family.

For Sigmund, by no means an ace, but by background and education having more in common with the middle-class technocrat Immelmann than with the aristocratic cavalryman Richthofen, the EKII was at the very least symbolic if not seminal. Whether the medal was earned for vanquishing an enemy or preserving an aircraft, the award represented two years during which his young life was at risk. It was no Blue Max, but to Sigmund it could be held in one hand, physical

---

[10] Wilkins, Mark, "The Dark Side of Glory, an Early Glimpse of PTSD in the Letters of World War I Aces," *Air & Space Smithsonian*, March 2018, pp. 54-59.

proof of a time in his life that left a profound indelible impression on him – the details of which were too deep and disturbing to share with his family.

CHAPTER THREE
"Troublesome Friends"[11]

The November 1918 Armistice brought the shooting war between Germany and the Entente Powers to an end, but the Armistice brought little relief from war for the Kiedrowski family. August, a *vizefeldwebel* (army staff sergeant), was reported missing two days before the Armistice; his remains were never found,

August Kiedrowski ca. 1918 (far left)

placing him among the over one million German combatants missing in action.[12] The surviving brothers were now being swept along in the postwar political flood tide that often turned violent.

The immediate results of the war were no less transformational for the brothers than for the rest of the world. No single event in their lifetimes affected them and their families more than World War I and its peace treaties. Their ancestral region had been part of the Kingdom of Prussia since 1772 as a result of the First Partition of Poland. Their

---

[11] Woodrow Wilson's remarks on the Poles during the Paris Peace Conference, despite his early championing of the restoration of the Polish state in the Fourteen Points.

[12] *Armee-Verordnungsblatt: Deutsche Verlustlisten, 1918*.11.09. Ausgabe 2203, p. 27613, accessed October 15, 2020, https://www.wbc.Poznan.pl/dlibra/publication/199013/edition/180923/content, p.9. The indicated place of birth, Berent, is correct, but the date of birth is given as 1 August, rather than 15 August (no birth year indicated in these lists).

father and grandfathers were born in Prussia. They were citizens of the Kingdom of Prussia, then of the German Empire after its creation in 1871. Five of the brothers, Sigmund, Klemens, Władysław, Anastazy and August served in the active military of the German Empire in World War I. As many as forty million soldiers and civilians were killed, likely including August, making the First World War a historical event of colossal proportions, but casualties were not the reason for its importance to the brothers. It was a matter of cultural identity. With so much effort put into creating nation-states with defined cultural identities, it was not surprising that cultural identity became an issue for the brothers as they sought to re-establish their disrupted lives, but despite growing Kashubian ethnic consciousness, there was no Kashubian state, only Poland or Germany for the Kiedrowski brothers.

The initial impact on Sigmund and his family was an experience for the most part shared by British, French and Belgian veterans on their homecoming. All were faced with property destruction, joblessness, and in some cases – especially in the territory of defeated Germany – hunger to the point of starvation. But there the similarities ended because Sigmund and his brothers returned to a new state formed from constituent parts of former empires. In most cases, the conclusion of the war meant that survivors could return home, but because the war ended just as suddenly as it began, the return, though expected, for many, was rarely immediate. Over the seven months between armistice and peace treaty, newly-demobilized veterans became forces in states often in political and social turmoil from the war, destabilizing some of them and spreading volatility across Europe.

Johann still lived in Essen with his wife and children, but like the other brothers in Poland, he and his family in Germany were faced with the internal social and political struggles and international conflicts that characterized their respective homelands. Sigmund and three of his brothers, Klemens, Władysław and Anastazy, could count themselves among the fortunate survivors of wartime service. They served actively and returned with considerable psychological baggage. Sigmund flew. Klemens related years later that as an infantryman, he escaped a gas attack. No one recalls that, in fact, he was wounded lightly twice in March of 1918, as recorded in the *Verlustlisten*. Władysław was captured and spent time as a prisoner of the British. He reportedly was an artillery observer in a gondola dangling beneath a balloon filled with hydrogen gas. Anastazy, drafted in 1915, served as a sapper until captured by the British in August 1918. Most remarkable is that Anton, at age 66, was wounded twice, once in May and again in October 1918. Their service made them veterans of an army that, in popular opinion, was defeated by its own leadership that surrendered to the Allies even though their home country was never invaded by the enemy, points that would be raised in the coming years by successor governments and opposition political parties.

The Armistice was a seismic shock – unexpected and intense. The Versailles Treaty was an aftershock of only slightly less magnitude. No longer were all the brothers citizens of the German Empire. Whether living in Poland or Germany, each of the brothers faced a fraught personal test. The war had put their lives on hold and now those in Poland faced new political and cultural realities defined by the new Second Polish Republic, with its bright promise, while Johann would experience challenges in the German Weimar Republic, the successor state to the collapsed and defeated Empire, the pariah nation of Europe.

Although the most obvious results of the war – death and devastation – passed in time, their impact endured in new boundaries as well as political and social systems, never far from consciousness every day for more than two decades, as the brothers' newly-reset lives moved on, often in unanticipated directions and more often than not colored by their wartime experiences.

———

A crucial provision of the Versailles Treaty created access to the Baltic Sea for the new Polish state. A "corridor" was created to link the bulk of the state to the Baltic, the so-called Polish Corridor, splitting East Prussia from the rest of Germany. As a result, what had been a united province of Prussia was now in three pieces: Pomerania (*Pommern* in German), the Polish Corridor and the Free City of Danzig. The corridor included areas mainly Polish in ethnicity, but with a large (as much as twenty percent) German minority. The Kiedrowski family home in Berent (now re-named Kościer-zyna) was included in the corridor. With a few strokes of a pen in Paris, the family's citizenship became Polish, after being Prussian, then German, for over a hundred and twenty years.

Although sharing some of the challenges Germany faced during the postwar period, such as a weak economy, Poland had some unique ones derived from its a hundred and twenty-three-year absence from the map of Europe. Poland's struggles to create a politically and administratively integrated nation-state were similar to those of the various nineteenth-century national unification efforts of Germany and Italy. The six simultaneous wars Poland waged during 1918-1921 were its wars of unification, as Poland attempted to include within its borders all people of Polish ethnicity. Characterized by one historian as "nursery brawls" among the infant states, campaigns included the Ukrainian War (1918-1919), the Posnanian War (1918-1919), the Silesian War (1919-1921), the Lithuanian War (1919-1920), the Czechoslovak War (1919-1920), and the Soviet War (1919-1922), this last the most challenging of them all.[13]

Fixed borders were not in place until 1922, after all the various conflicts had been concluded. However, fixing borders did not solve the one issue with which the SPR struggled through its entire existence: minority nationalities. More than thirty percent of the population was not of Polish ancestry. The minorities included Germans, Ukrainians, Byelorussians, Russians, Jews and Lithuanians.[14] With the exception of the Jews, the minorities were concentrated along the borders with like nationalities in the adjoining states. Many now within Poland wished to return to and/or join their fellow ethnic group across the border, and in the case of the German minority, they were openly hostile, even violent about their desire to leave Poland. This situation was anticipated by the diplomats at Versailles, and they forced Poland to sign a Polish Minority Treaty in 1919, which was essentially confirmed in the Constitution of March 17, 1921. The government rarely followed the prescribed treatment of minorities, but arguably did better than governments in Germany and Soviet Russia.

What the brothers and all veterans on all sides wanted most of all was a return to a normal life, whatever that might be in light of new political realities, but for the brothers, the old normalcy of Prussian hegemony – for all its negatives – had vanished, and so had its social, political and cultural stability. The physical structures of their homes were still there, but the context had changed. They were struggling with what amounted to loss of place in this new society with its new life rules.

It was not so much the promise of peace as the re-creation of the Polish state as largely dictated by the Treaty of Versailles that would be more crucial than any other factor for the

---

[13] Norman Davies, *God's Playground: A History of Poland.* 2 vols. (New York: Columbia University Press, 2005). Vol II, p. 292.

[14] The Kashubians were not considered a minority nationality.

brothers' respective futures. Unlike the French and British veterans who returned to war-ravaged countries but with political and economic institutions relatively intact, the Kiedrowski brothers now faced what was nothing less than new rules for living in a state with a variety of social and political traditions that had become deeply ingrained over the years of the partitions.

Even with attempts to set borders based on ethnicity, there was the inevitable opposition, especially with regard to the border between Germany and Poland. For example, part of one border fell within an area inhabited by large numbers of Kashubs, an area referred to as *Gochy*, a term Kashubs in the area used to refer to themselves in the Catholic parish of Borzyszkowy. The area included Kiedrowice, among other villages. In the spring of 1919, the local press leaked to the public where the border between Poland and Germany was going to be laid out. The area was destined to be turned over entirely to Germany's province of Pomerania, but census figures from 1892 revealed all of the villages were predominantly Kashubian in ethnic makeup. The regional government in Poland appointed representatives and sent them to plead their case to the peacemakers in Paris. The Germans had claimed that the inhabitants were not Poles, so they should not be included within the Polish borders. The *Gochy* representatives presented a petition stating that not only were they "Poles, but our fathers had also been Poles and their ancestors had lived in the area since time immemorial, and that land belonged to Poland." The Kashubian majority in the region stated their position not as Kashubs, but as Poles who wanted to live in the new Polish state. Although this assertion of Polish citizenship was happening at the same time as the Society of Young Kashubians (*Towarzystwo Młodokaszubskie*) established in 1912, was growing in popularity,[15] the protesters' position with regard to ethnicity was clearly expressed to leave no ambiguity in that binary world of recognized nationalities in the region. Had they asserted Kashubian nationality or citizenship, there would have been no change in the borders, since there was no Kashubian state under consideration, and if they were not Poles, the only option was to be included in Germany. It was black and white. In this area, if you were not Polish, you would live in Germany.

There was a practical issue as well. The new German-Polish border divided *Gochy* into two parts, and in many cases, farmers would be cut off from the meadows, fields and forests they had used for generations. Tending livestock, plowing fields or collecting products from the forest could require passing through German border control. After experiencing German rule for over a century, having to battle a hostile, entrenched anti-Catholic German bureaucracy to enter their fields on a regular basis proved too much to bear.

On February 16, 1920, German troops came to enforce the division of the Kashubian lands and were immediately confronted by an angry mob of at least one thousand villagers at Lake Star *(Jezioro Gwiazda)*. The demonstrators had been called to action by notices posted in the various villages on February 12. Polish troops were also in the area. Shots were fired (reportedly in the air). Although away from the protest some negotiations had already begun between the parties, surveyors started hammering in the stakes that would indicate the location of the permanent concrete border markers. As fast as the surveyors pounded in the stakes, the villagers pulled them out. It became known as the "stakes war" (*Wojna*

---

[15] Józef Borzyszkowski, *The Kashubs, Pomerania and Gdańsk.* Translated by Tomasz Wicherkiewicz. (Gdańsk: Kashubian Institute in Gdańsk, 2005) p. 146.

Palikowa).[16] Eventually, a newly-agreed-upon delineation from Paris was transmitted through local channels via the International Boundary Commission in Toruń, Poland. The border was moved as much as 10 km westward from what the surveyors had attempted to lay out. The final determination of this particular section of the border was not accomplished until May 1920. And this was just one area of contention. The border wars on other fronts, especially in the regions of Lithuania in the northeast and Galicia in the southeast, would, in fact, last until 1923 and often were settled with less civility and a greater loss of life.

Kashubian ethnic consciousness became invigorated by the creation of the Second Republic, which they embraced, but the community was divided by the corridor, with some Kashubs in German Pomerania, some in the corridor, and some in Danzig. Any attempt to consolidate was met with

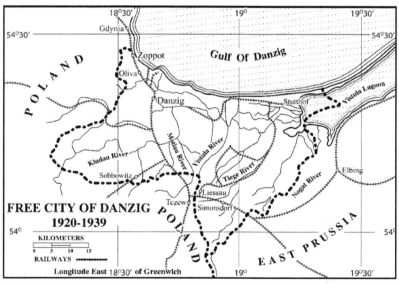

---

[16] The phrase *wojna palikowa* was popularized by Zbigniew Talewski. See http://www.naszekaszuby.pl/modules/artykuly/article.php?articleid=261 by Andrzej Szutowicz. The event is commemorated in February with a march by the residents of the village of Borowy Mlyn.

suspicion by Germany and/or Poland. The assertion of Polish citizenship seemed not to alter Kashubian cultural struggles even within the Polish state. Germany saw the Kashubs as a possible wedge into weakening Poland, and intelligence services of Poland in the 1930s surveilled the Kashubian activists, fearing them to be a pro-German force that could impede Polish access to the sea through the corridor.[17]

Created in November 1920, the quasi-independent Free City of Danzig was under the protection of the League of Nations. In its long history since 997, it had been a member of the Hanseatic League, and for several hundred years, the chief shipping point of eastern European grain to Western Europe. Ethnically, it had been predominantly German. That had not changed by the early twentieth century.

It was, in fact, a small state, comprising over 1800 square km, more than twice the area of today's city-state of Singapore. It included several towns and hundreds of hamlets and villages stretching eastward, south and a bit west of the city proper. About 40 km of the lower course of the Vistula was also included in the city. It bordered East Prussia on the east and the corridor on the west. It had a land border of more than 160 km, but none with the largest portion of Germany, and that fact, together with the isolation of East Prussia, would become a major impetus and rallying cry in Hitler's plans for a new Europe.

Although Danzig proper was overwhelmingly (ninety percent) German, the free city surrounding it was predominantly Polish, just as the corridor itself was no more than twenty percent German, including such cities as Kościerzyna and Grudziądz, which were also predominantly Polish, but with 18.6% and 27.8% German minorities, respectively.[18] In

---

[17] Borzyszkowski, *The Kashubs, Pomerania and Gdańsk*, p. 119.
[18] In calculations of ethnicity in the plebiscites Kashubs were not distinguished from Poles.

creating the free city, the Versailles Treaty established even more friction points between the Germans and the Poles (and the Kashubs, for many of whom it was an unofficial capital). Because of issues it experienced in loading ships in Danzig, Poland established a facility on Westerplatte, a heavily wooded island which for years had been used as a park and recreation area, but when Poland continued to have difficulties even after that, a port was established in Gdynia, a small fishing village and tourist destination to the north, which soon became much busier than Danzig. The Free City had its own postal system, but the Poles deemed necessary the creation of a local office for the Polish postal system. There were competing mail boxes in the city – just one more friction point. And as though there wasn't enough confusion, the free city was represented abroad by the Polish ambassadors to the various countries.

The restoration of the Polish state was an event of great excitement for many, anger for some, and confusion for most. It created new borders to cross, complicating the everyday activities that for many years had been relatively effortless within the German Empire. Commerce became disrupted by the variety of currencies that were now introduced. Poland, Germany and The Free City of Danzig each had its own monetary, postage and customs systems. In fact, East Prussia had its own currency, and even some cities, for example Allenstein (Olsztyn) in East Prussia, issued their own paper money. Trains that in the past traveled unhindered from Berlin to Königsberg in East Prussia now had to pass through the corridor over two more borders with the potential for delay that entailed. Even sealing passenger cars by Polish authorities so that travelers from Berlin to Königsberg could not leave their cars in the corridor and hence would not need a visa for Poland led to substantial delays.

The creation of the Polish Republic was a stunning occurrence for the Kiedrowski family – and for the population of Europe in general. But for Poles, the creation of the corridor and the continuing presence of Prussia on the borders of northern Poland constituted a malevolent spirit of German cultural presence still lurking as an incubus. Add to that a crusading Bolshevik government to the east, and there continued to fester a geo-political crisis not seen in more than a century. Even when military action ceased, and borders were re-drawn, they were impermanent and often subject to new military action to enforce or modify political agreements.

———

Discharge of April 15, 1919

Deactivated with the Armistice, Sigmund returned to Graudenz on January 25, 1919. Shortly after that, on February 15, he was enrolled in FA(A) 215 (*Fliegerabteilung (Artillerie) – Flying Unit, Artillery*) – at the Graudenz military airbase. That group was a border defense (*Grenzschutz*) unit. For the next two months, he served in that unit until his formal military discharge on April 15, when he finished service in FEA 8. The year 1919 was a year of widespread political and social unrest throughout Europe, with revolutionary fervor reaching well into the military, so in addition to the unit commander, the head of the soldiers' revolutionary council (*Soldatenrat*) of the Graudenz airbase signed off on his discharge. Now no longer in military service, Sigmund stayed at the Graudenz base until May 26, working as a civilian repairman of "all sorts" of instruments and watches. The shop closed and Sigmund was forced to seek new employment, but his training as a watchmaker had stood him in good stead as his military career wound down. He had managed to parlay his two skills – watchmaking and flying – into the position at Graudenz. Unfortunately, the closure of the instrument shop put him on the road again in search of work, a week after the publication of the harsh terms of the Treaty of Versailles that were intended to crush not only the German military, but the German economy as well.

Border defense groups like the unit at Graudenz were part of the *Freikorps*, created by the German defense minister primarily to put down the Bolshevik threat in Germany proper, especially in East Prussia and the Baltics, and to prevent Polish seizures of territory in Silesia and East Prussia. Graudenz's significant distance from Silesia in the southwest suggests FA(A) 215 was concerned mainly with German interests in East Prussia. The *Freikorps* was largely made up of officers who saw their lives of privilege about to disappear in the new democratic Weimar Republic. Counterbalancing them on the left were Bolshevik sympathizers who saw Weimar as not going far enough to crush the anti-democratic forces of aristocracy and privilege.

Now out of work, Sigmund's personal contacts from his short military career seemed a natural source to network for opportunities. Since there was military activity in East Prussia (a staunchly German cultural area) being undertaken by *Freikorps* units, it was natural for him to explore opportunities there. One contact he had there appeared prominently in his address book from several years later as "Rittergutsbesitzer von Conta, Schwarzwald krs. Sensburg" (Lord of the Black Forest Manor von Conta, Sensburg region).[19] The presence in East Prussia of former airman Gottlieb Ewald Joachim von Conta (1897-1978) opened up some employment possibilities to explore. Von Conta was the youngest son of Richard Heinrich Karl von Conta, a Major General of the Prussian infantry in the war. Von Conta could also give Sigmund an entrée into a class of people that had at least traditionally been more able to afford luxury items like watches and jewelry in this land of large estates and wealthy landowners – but was now impoverished after a devastating war. This acquaintance may have gone back to their service in the same air unit during WWI. Just two years older than Sigmund, von Conta (a Lieutenant), began service in Jasta 11 in February 1918 after serving in FA-36, about the time or shortly after Sigmund completed pilot training. Whether they both served in Jasta 11, the unit served in by such Luftstreitskräfte luminaries as the von Richthofen brothers and uncle, Ernst Udet and Hermann Göring, is uncertain. Von Conta's service is almost as obscure as Sigmund's.

The job search that began in May concluded successfully in September 1919 when Sigmund found a position in East Prussia, far to the east in the city of Lyck, a job that would shape his future to an extraordinary degree. On September 9,

---

[19] Von Conta was the top entry of the first page in the address section of Sigmund's 1925 calendar. The entry of another resident of East Prussia, Otto von Strauhs [sic] of Königsberg, was just beneath von Conta. Strauhs does not appear on pilot lists from WWI. These were the only two addresses in East Prussia that Sigmund recorded those years later. More on the 1925 calendar and its mysteries is revealed in the next chapter.

"Herr Sigismund v. Loewe-Kiedrowski" started a job with Ernst Klüppelholz, a jeweler with a shop at 17 Hindenburg-strasse. Lyck's population was ninety-nine percent German, according to the League of Nations plebiscite. For whatever reason, Sigmund, more than Władysław, Klemens or Anastazy, gravitated toward Germany, rather than to the new Poland, just as his brother Johann had done more than a decade earlier when he settled in Essen.

Sigmund's move to East Prussia coincided with continuing conflict in the area as Poland attempted to reclaim territory in its eastern regions that had been in the Russian Partition. Józef Piłsudski, the head of the new Polish state and commander of its military (and former political prisoner of Tsarist Russia), expected that Poland eventually would have to defend its existence against a Bolshevik Russia, and that the opposition to the Bolsheviks had even less interest than the Bolsheviks in maintaining an independent Polish state. The White opposition consisted largely of monarchists and other aristocrats who had exploited Poles during the time of the Partitions.

Poland's war with Soviet Russia and Ukraine was ended by the Treaty of Riga on March 18, 1920, clearly defining the eastern borders of Poland as they would be for the next two decades. But it was a triumph that contained yet another challenge with potentially huge consequences for the government. Together with Poles, the territories conquered included a bycatch of Ukrainians, Byelorussians and Lithuanians, and when added to sizable minorities of Jews and Germans, Poland now had a thirty percent minority population within their multi-ethnic state with its three distinct social, political and economic traditions deeply ingrained over the years of the partitions. It was an unenviable situation to have inside its eastern borders large concentrations of non-Poles at the same time as it was forced to coexist side-by-side with the Free City of Danzig and East Prussia in the north with their large and perpetually antagonistic

German populations. To many included in those minority populations, the Polish government and its Catholic faith were considered an anathema and a permanent provocation which called for resistance.

The new Polish republic bore all the characteristics of a nation of migrants, rather than a nation-state unified in ethnicity as the diplomats at Paris had intended, and the Kiedrowski family was no exception. The place they had known since birth as West Prussia, part of the German Empire, was now part of a newly-constituted Polish state. The language banned from schools and government for generations by government decree almost overnight was now their primary language. Cultural differences alien to the majority of Poles in the fledgling country were now widespread among the non-Poles folded into the new republic by military action.

The presence of a large minority of migrants created by the aggressive defense and extension of its borders did not augur well for Poland and its policy of ethnolinguistic homogenization, the multi-ethnic reality falling far short of the re-unification dream. The disappointing results of efforts to re-unite Poles beyond its borders with their homeland, coupled with the attempt to keep Bolshevism at bay laid the groundwork for the catastrophe that would stagger even the most distant family members.

Sigmund worked for Klüppelholz in Lyck for little more than a year, and on November 1, 1920, disappeared into the continuing maelstrom.

CHAPTER FOUR
Pivot

Sigmund's Germany was in complete chaos. Political violence and revolution convulsed government and super-heated inflation devastated the economy even before Allied demands for reparations threatened its complete collapse. Strikes and unemployment became common. The middle class was being crushed between post-war tycoons and proletarianized workers. His good fortune in finding professional employment in the fall of 1919 came to an end thirteen months later without any cause stated in the letter of reference as he left Klüppelholz on October 31, 1920. His professional and personal life over the next two years is largely a mystery, but his disappearance in late 1920 was more apparent than real, related solely to an unusual absence of documents. Up to then, most of his activities, training, employment, and military service were reported with at least some certain dates of beginning or end. Sigmund retained many documents, including letters of reference, certification of watchmaking skill, identity documents, and some unmarked photos, all held neatly in a passport case.

His absence from documents for nearly two years came at a time of considerable turmoil throughout Europe. But during that time, he became engaged in business activities on his own account as an entrepreneur, and those activities were so important or formative to him and so indelibly etched in his memory, that he recorded them more than three years later, enciphered and encoded.

As a journeyman watchmaker, Sigmund was well ac-quainted with precious stones. For two hundred years they had been used as bearings in clocks and watches, prized for their low friction and high durability, and since ancient times larger stones had been worn as a display of wealth. Even utilitarian objects from pre-literate societies were occasionally decorated with them. But in the world of rubies, emeralds and sapphires, no gemstone was more valuable, dramatic and worthy of his attention than billion-year-old carbon crystals – diamonds. Sought by princes, kings and emperors since time immemorial, they captured and held his attention his whole life and played the featured role in one of the great mysteries that he created.

The sale of diamonds was and is even today carefully managed. The price paid at retail, twice the wholesale price, is said to be the gross margin. The difference between retail and wholesale is called the "keystone price". It is today almost impossible to sell back to a jeweler a cut diamond for more than sixty percent of wholesale; the keystone price *plus* is lost to the original buyer, now the hopeful seller. Compared to the political, social and cultural turmoil that followed the war, events in Africa in the 1860s could hardly have seemed important enough to affect Sigmund's life, but developments that followed the discovery of diamonds in South Africa in 1867 would figure prominently in his business and professional life, and would persist with worldwide impact into the twenty-first century.

According to Sigmund's notes made nearly four years later, around the middle of October 1920, while he was still employed by Klüppelholz, he became involved in a transaction in loose diamonds initiated by unknown parties. There had been a substantial decline in diamond value during the war as demand dried up. With their history of wide swings in value, Sigmund sought to profit from the expected recovery of prewar value. He finalized the purchase on or about November 10. Since he no longer worked for Klüppelholz, nor for any other employer as far as can be determined, it was an independent undertaking. By late March 1921, he was in possession of several carats of diamonds, source unknown, and apparently in early April tried without success to sell them. Two years later, he brought those same loose stones with him to America. If Sigmund, in his youthful (age twenty-one) entrepreneurial spirit, hoped to make a living dealing in diamonds, he may have become disillusioned by the course and outcome of this transaction, but it was at least a learning experience.

The dates and rough outline of the failed deal appear in a 1925 pocket calendar of his, most likely copied from his notes for unknown reasons. A promotional piece distributed by the Charles Beard Company of St. Paul, Minnesota, a wholesale jeweler and supplier, the calendar probably was in Sigmund's hands not much before September of 1924, more than a year after his arrival in America. Pocket calendars like this one traditionally were distributed to jewelers close to the end of the year, but well in advance of Christmas to generate business for the wholesaler (see Appendix II, The Diamond Cipher).

The enciphered, encoded entries achieved Sigmund's intent. The events memorialized remain a mystery to this day, more than a century later. This enterprise over the period of six months does little really to explain conclusively the whole eighteen-month gap in the documents he carefully kept for decades. His secret was safe, but perhaps served as a cautionary reminder for him of dealing with the growing De Beers diamond cartel or its agents, especially during times of political and social uncertainty, with borders still in flux in Poland, radical uprisings throughout Germany, and civil war in Russia.

Coinciding with Sigmund's blurry employment picture during this period was another unusual phenomenon. Faced with the revolution burning throughout Germany, and hobbled by limited military resources sanctioned by Versailles, in 1920, the German government allowed pilots and the few remaining planes not yet destroyed or confiscated by Allied authorities to be assigned to police units to quell disturbances caused by the soldier and worker revolutionary councils. Some returning pilots found employment in that newly formed *Luftpolizei* (air police) for a brief period after the war, starting in March of 1920. Not part of the *Freikorps* phenomenon, the activity was more police than military in nature. It afforded some of the hundreds of demobilized and unemployed pilots and observers jobs using their talents and experience. These were opportunities for those veteran pilots like Sigmund, who were struggling to find employment in the new civilian economy. It would allow Sigmund to use his flying skills at a time when the demand for jewelers and watchmakers was at a low ebb. Most of the units had both pilots and observers, and the support staff was not that much different from the military air units of World War I, which often numbered among their one hundred or so personnel, not only mechanics, but cobblers, carpenters and canvas menders, but that was a far cry from providing employment for all those veterans who needed it.

Among others, in the spring of 1920, there was an air police squadron (thirty planes, including one bomber, converted to a civilian transport) at Allenstein, approximately 120 km from Sigmund's job in Lyck in East Prussia. A much larger squadron (forty-three planes, also including one bomber/transport) was at Königsberg. More distant, but still in East Prussia.

The activities carried out by the air police varied from crowd control during political uprisings to criminal investigations. For example, the Karlshorst squadron in Berlin from November 7, 1920, to February 23, 1921, had ninety-seven calls for security purposes and thirty-six calls for criminal acts. In fact, on October 15, 1920 (the time of the first diamond cipher entry by Sigmund), three investigating officers used a twin-engine bomber/transport to fly to the occupied Rhineland territory to investigate an incident involving smuggled diamonds and stolen securities. It is tempting to read something more than coincidence into the

October 15 date of diamond smuggler pursuit and that first entry of the enciphered notes. There is no evidence that the two actions were related beyond calendar, but the incident does illustrate that diamonds were a commodity in demand as government currency lost value. The air police squadrons were essentially disbanded in May 1921 (a month after the last entry of the enciphered notes), eliminating even that limited opportunity for veteran airmen.

Until he left for America in the spring of 1923, after he left Klüppelholz in November of 1920, Sigmund resided in Sensburg, East Prussia. After living in Lyck, very close to the old Russian Empire that was being devastated by civil war and the resultant flight of often-wealthy opponents of the Bolshevik regime, he must have regarded Sensburg as something of a sanctuary. It was located to the west of Lyck and east of Allenstein, in the Masurian Lakes district. As noted in the preceding chapter, his presence in East Prussia may have been linked to service during the war with von Conta, a resident of Sensburg. The von Conta address book entry suggests that Sigmund had some sort of relationship perhaps more recent than the war, such as might have been the case had he sought out von Conta during his years in East Prussia. It was recent enough in memory to include that former pilot in his address book after immigrating to America.

Sigmund's residency in East Prussia may have raised some eyebrows among his three brothers who remained in the Second Republic, but their brother Johann still lived in Germany and these were challenging times that often forced individuals to accept circumstances they were not entirely comfortable with. Germany had lost the war, but Poland was a besieged nation on all sides, and armed conflict was not over. All the brothers, except for Johann, had actively served in the German forces during World War I. All had sufficient language skills and fluency to work whichever side of whatever border they were near, but the fluidity of borders and the equally fluid if not volatile political situation within Poland (no less so in Germany), made even daily life challenging for anyone who just stepped out their front door. Political assassination and street violence were common. But more than the confusion and uncertainty of the conditions, the brothers were often faced with choices and even opportunities that they had never encountered before. Those choices, largely Hobsonian in nature, were forced on them by the war, armistice and the peace treaty.

After Sigmund presumably left Lyck in November of 1920, there are no preserved documents until a Polish ID (*wykaz osobisty* – see in Prologue) of May 6, 1922, identifies him as a resident of Kościerzyna (formerly known as Berent). Although he is in Danzig the next day, he would have been able to attend the wedding of his brother, Anastazy, and Zofia Majkowski on May 9. Although Sigmund is absent from the only surviving wedding photo, it is likely he was in attendance, as was Klemens, whose almost imperious posture is clearly visible. He's back in Sensburg in November, but with the exception of frequent trips to Danzig, including around Christmas, Sensburg remained Sigmund's primary residence from November 1920 until he left for America in the spring of 1923.

The Polish identity document Sigmund obtained in May stipulated that he was a resident of Kościerzyna, of Polish nationality (*narodowość*) with Polish citizenship (*przynależność panstw)* – the last extant document identifying him as Polish. In it his profession is still noted as watchmaker. He used that ID on several occasions to travel back and forth to Danzig. However, he had also a German travel pass (*Reise-Pass*), issued in Sensburg, East Prussia on November 21, 1922, good for one year. Both contained entries when he traveled to Danzig in December of that year, allowing him to cross the border of East Prussia into Danzig. In addition, the Polish ID allowed him to enter and cross the corridor without a Polish visa, since he was a citizen of Poland as well.

During these two years of mystery, and really until he emigrated in the spring of 1923, although Sigmund's employment is not recorded, what has been passed down in his documents is an undated photo of sixteen men and six women in what has been identified by one family member as a police office with his brother Anastazy standing in the front row right (circled), and Sigmund standing next to the end on the left in the back (circled), in a uniform tunic similar to what he would have worn when an airman in the German air service. Anastazy served continuously for nearly twenty years in the national police in Toruń from July 1, 1920. Whether policeman or air-policeman, Sigmund's career in uniform would be short and not even in his homeland, much less in occupied Germany like Johann, but far away from family and his roots.

Decades later, when asked why he left the "old country", with a wink and smile, Sigmund would respond, "I had to stay ahead of the sheriff". When pressed for a more serious answer, he never expressed any reason other than the economic conditions of Europe in 1923. But his decision to leave family and friends to immigrate to the United States could not have been made lightly, though in these early years he enjoyed the financial and personal support of his brothers and parents, support clearly recorded in the pocket calendar for 1925. Twenty years later, emigration would catapult him from the youngest and least established of the family to caretaker and family counselor.

Prompted by the lack of employment after he left Graudenz, then the move to Lyck, followed by his unsuccessful entrepreneurial dalliance with diamonds, what had been a simple job search took on a far broader meaning for the veteran. It became a life change on a magnitude of his wartime service, an experience that already had reset his life while in his teens like millions of others. Finding a job abroad was far more complicated, however, for not only did he need to secure the promise of employment via the international mail service of that time, but also to arrange travel across the Atlantic and an unfamiliar country to the job. It was a staggering undertaking.

From 1922 to 1927, Sigmund left many clues to his travels, some intentional, but like those left by a rabbit moving through a wood in winter, there are clear tracks, but few revealed motivations. Why exactly he made the decision to leave his home and when that commitment was made are unknown. His travel documents pinpoint movements in time and place while he was in Poland, Germany and Danzig. His arrival in America is documented, as is the sequence of jobs he held subsequent to that watershed event. Newspaper clippings from the time of his early residence in America add some color, but his black and white snapshots create more questions than answers.

If a stumbling economy and personal financial pressures attributable to it were not sufficient to steer Sigmund ultimately to the United States, the political situation in Poland and Germany gave little reason to stay. Even though the employment opportunities in East Prussia were by 1923 proving disappointing, at least the political situation was more stable. By contrast, from its very inception, the government of Poland lurched from crisis to crisis. The assassination of the president, Gabriel Narutowicz in December of 1922, just five days after his election by the National Assembly as the first president of the Second Polish Republic could hardly inspire confidence in the new republic.

An obvious choice in terms of cultural familiarity was a state of Weimar Germany west of the Polish Corridor, but it was an even less attractive option than Poland. Political violence was even more widespread in Germany, demonstrated by the *Freikorps* and the other right-wing ethnic-nationalist groups in opposition to Bolshevik influence. He was a citizen of the divided Free State of Prussia, a representative democracy, but that province, making up over sixty percent of Germany's landmass and population and being the location of Germany's capital, Berlin, was divided by the Polish Corridor. Sigmund was close to his eldest brother, Johann, who lived in Essen, Germany, and probably relied on his counsel more than on that of their father, now almost seventy years old. Johann was able to relate to Sigmund the equally dire conditions in his region of Germany, especially with the two- and one-half-year occupation of the Ruhr by French and Belgian troops that commenced in January 1923. Had the war turned out differently, perhaps Sigmund would have joined his brother in the Essen area like some cousins had done years earlier. But having heard from an experienced and trusted source how bad things were in Germany beyond the corridor, it was more prudent to head for a country with greater promise and less turmoil. Sigmund sought to leave behind the gloomy economic and political realities of postwar Europe.

The United States was the only major power not to have suffered enormous casualties. Its combined military deaths from all causes totaled little more than a hundred thousand, compared to over a million each for France, Great Britain, and

Austria-Hungary, and over two million for Germany. Nor had it sustained any physical damage. It also had an economy that not only was not in shambles but by 1923 was growing after stumbling briefly in the 1920-1921 recession. The old aristocracy of Europe had been largely swept out of power or totally impoverished by the war. America had a new aristocracy, one with wealth that could be shared by those who provided the luxury goods they sought. Moreover, there were many German communities in America that could offer Sigmund the promise of a familiar language and culture. That aspect of being a migrant – the loss of language – at least was not an overriding issue, even though he was faced with learning English, which he had never formally studied or even spoken before arrival. In the short term, he could survive in a German immigrant community. The American culture was unfamiliar to him, but he could adapt. His home was behind him, but he would find a new one. However, there were no close family members in the U.S., not even distant cousins; there was no familial safety net for this young immigrant. Whatever his motivation for leaving home for America, for the rest of his life he never voiced a shred of regret for coming to the United States, and his decision was validated repeatedly during the years to come.

Originally drawn by the promise of employment in East Prussia and after spending more than two years there, Anastazy and Zofia's wedding celebration in 1922 provided an opportunity for him to discuss with his family his proposed emigration. It was not unusual for lively family discussions to take on the character of a debate with these young men, and their conversations lasted long into the night, as they always seemed to, doubtless marked by well-lubricated conviviality. Sigmund's parents may have preferred that he stay, while Johann, from his first-hand experience, may have encouraged him to emigrate, but not to the Germany beyond the corridor.

Sigmund's pivotal decision to immigrate to America

rather than to remain in Poland or Germany was further complicated by the virulent and widespread nativism of the time, clearly reflected in the U.S. immigration acts of 1921 and 1922. He could claim both Polish and German citizenship and nationality. In his Polish internal ID of May 6, 1922, as Zygmund Kiedrowski, his nationality is noted as Polish, as is his citizenship. Less than seven months later, on November 21,

1922, he was issued a German passport, signing it as S.v.Loewe Kiedrowski, resident of Sensburg (a city ninety-nine percent German). He had spent a year in Lyck, close to the border with the Soviet Union, which was experiencing substantial population flight to Germany and France in particular as a result of its devastating civil war. By the spring of 1923, after pursuing different options and experiencing setbacks and obstacles to a clear and consistent career path through the thicket of postwar turmoil, a course had been selected by the twenty-four-year-old journeyman watchmaker, failed diamond trader and erstwhile pilot. In April, back again in Sensburg, he would receive the most important letter of his life, one that would create the stunning course correction turning him from East Prussia westward to

America.

On March 27, 1923, John Gaschk had written a letter promising employment addressed to Sigmund in Sensburg, East Prussia, Germany. Sigmund wrote the date April 20 on the envelope. Gaschk wrote in German:

> "Dear Friend Sigismund: I am sending you today a ticket and am very happy that you want to come over here. Hopefully, you won't encounter any difficulties on the way, but if you need something, send me a telegram or write me. My address is John Gaschk, Wishek, N.Dak. Best regards, Your Friend, John Gaschk."

The envelope from Gaschk clearly confirms Sigmund's continuing presence in Sensburg. That is the mailing address Gaschk knew would find Sigmund, not his hometown of Kościerzyna or his prior place of employment in Lyck. Within two weeks of receiving the letter on April 20, Sigmund was on his way to take advantage of this invitation from someone who had considerable recent experience with the process of immigration to America.

Gaschk, then 49, was living with his widowed mother, Amelia, who was in her seventies. She and her husband, Daniel, of Eichmedien, East Prussia (now Nakomiady, Poland), had arrived in the U.S. on May 16, 1910. She had been widowed by 1920 and was living with her son John, but when she and her husband passed through Ellis Island, their destination was Dogden, North Dakota, to be with another son, Paul. Both Gaschk and his mother had been born in Germany. Renting in Wishek, North Dakota, John was a watchmaker by trade and had immigrated to the U.S. in 1901 from Eichmedien, about 15 km from Sensburg.

Just the year before, Gaschk had paid the way for his niece Lydia Gaschk and nephew Willy Gaschk (both coming from Sensburg), who arrived in November 1922. Restrictions on immigration to the United States were increasing dramatically for those who originated in countries identified as undesirable, or those who were Jewish or Catholic. Gaschk may have sensed the urgency for bringing relatives into America in anticipation of the gate being closed – even for those of German ethnicity, "a Nordic race" favored by the eugenicists. The job Sigmund had found in 1919 in Lyck with Klüppelholz proved to have implications far beyond employment, even though it did not continue past November of 1920. The move to Sensburg proved to be crucial in his life. His road to America passed through East Prussia.

With the job offer in his passport case, he left Danzig on April 27, 1923, and took the train to Kościerzyna, where he said his goodbyes and posed for a somber studio photo with

1923, L-R: Władysław, Klemens, Sigmund, Anastazy

brothers Anastazy, Klemens and Władysław. He returned to Danzig two days later, on April 29 and then a week later, on May 7, he boarded a train at the main railroad station in Danzig and left behind not only East Prussia and the Free City of Danzig but his hometown of Kościerzyna (not to mention a couple of nationalities) and his family, crossing two borders before he entered Germany again.

Sigmund's first stop was Essen where his brother Johann and his family lived. He crossed into the Ruhr area that since January had been occupied by French and Belgian forces. On the back of a group photo, he carried in his passport case were hand-written instructions on how to request permission for a journey to

"Danzig, Berlin and the occupied areas".[20] The situation he observed in the occupied area could not help but confirm the wisdom of his decision to go to America.

Johann had been employed by the Essen public transit authority for a dozen years already, and the family was tightly packed into a flat in a building at 25 Katzenbruchstrasse, with Johann, Leocadia and their four children. For Sigmund to be surrounded by all these youngsters was not an entirely unfamiliar situation. He was the youngest of his siblings, and although of the brothers only Johann and Anastazy were married, their sister Maria had three children by this time – Jan aged six, Jadwiga aged nine and Elzibeta aged twelve. He was greeted at 25 Katzenbruchstrasse by four more pre-teen nieces and nephews: Irmgard aged seven, Hans aged eleven, Hildegard aged twelve, and Heinz, who had just turned two. It was a houseful, and not easy to feed and clothe in postwar occupied Germany in economic crisis. They had moved to this larger home in 1912, shortly after Hans was born, but now it was reaching capacity and full of activity as everyone doted on the toddler, who happily accepted being spoiled by his brother and sisters.

After spending two weeks with Johann and his family, Sigmund traveled to Hamburg in time to board with over four hundred other passengers the Royal Mail Steam Packet Company's SS *Orbita*, a coal-fired steamship of the Royal Mail Steam Packet Company, built in 1914 by Harlan & Wolff Limited, Belfast, the builders of the RMS *Titanic*. Sigmund's voyage to America was by far a more propitious one. The *Orbita* had been viewed by its operator as a good investment

---

[20] It reads in German "Betrifft: Gesuch um Ausstellung eines Reisepasses. Unterzeichner bitte höflich um geneigte Ausstellung eines Reisepasses zwecks einer Reise nach Danzig, Berlin und den bestezten Gebieten." It is unknown who wrote the instructions, but Johann was familiar with the situation.

for what promised to be the post-war revival of the profitable enterprise of carrying immigrants from Europe to America, but they couldn't have picked a worse time to start the service – April 1921, one month before the Emergency Quota Act was signed by President Warren G. Harding, limiting immigration to America.

Leaving Hamburg on May 23, the *Orbita* with Sigmund on board landed in New York on June 4, 1923, after scheduled stops in Cherbourg, France and Southampton, England. Sigmund – or "Sigismund Kiedrowski" as he was listed on the ship's manifest – was admitted to the U.S. on June 5, identified as a German from Sensburg, his most recent city of residence.

Sigmund was to join Gaschk in Wishek, seeking permanent residence, and was noted by the immigration officer as having been born in Germany in the town of Berent. This begs the question of whether he would have been admitted so freely had he displayed a Polish passport and a birthplace of Kościerzyna, Poland, especially bearing such an eastern European name. Given American immigration law and practices, the question is easily answered in the negative. By 1923 the welcome mat had been pulled, and the open door was quickly swinging shut on immigrants from southern and eastern Europe.

There was great fear at all levels of American society that "undesirables" might overwhelm the United States, making it a refuge for the world's most awful citizens (usually meaning Catholics and Jews from southern and eastern Europe, not to mention "Reds" and anarchists). That dread was a reflection of the widespread anti-immigration sentiment now fueled to a firestorm by the dubious science of eugenics advanced by some of the leading biologists and geneticists of the time. The immigration quota system the United States put into effect in June of 1921 marked the beginning of the end of open borders for immigrants to America. That act slashed immigration that was just re-starting after World War I had brought it to a halt, creating a major change in American policy that, when codified in the Immigration Act of 1924 (The Johnson-Reed Act), would severely restrict immigration on the basis of national origins until 1965.

By that act of 1921, just three percent of the total U.S.-resident foreign-born citizens of each nationality listed in the 1910 Census could be admitted each year. If there were one million Polish-born citizens in the U.S., then just thirty thousand could be admitted each year. One problem in calculating Poles in America was that there had been no real state of Poland since 1795. There were, of course, a "German Poland", an "Austrian Poland", and a "Russian Poland". In the past, Poles from the Russian Partition were considered Russian citizens, not Poles. The parsing of geography and splitting of national hairs, not to mention ethnicity and even religion, could put someone on a ship back to where they came from if the quota for their national or religious group was already filled. Many U.S. residents of Polish origin were not identified as such, and as a consequence, the Polish quota was abysmally small; there were few opportunities under the immigration law of 1921 for citizens of Poland to come in under quota. In fact, one month after the act was signed, thousands of Poles were stranded in the port of Antwerp, as the new percentages were applied to those who wanted to board a steamer to America.[21] And these numbers were based not solely on specific nationality but on citizenship. Immigration from Poland was cut by seventy percent by this act. The Immigration Act of 1924 became even more restrictive. Based on the Census of 1890, prior to the huge influx of eastern and southern Europeans that followed, it also reduced the three percent quota to two percent for each nationality group. For citizens of certain countries for all practical

---

[21] "3,000 Emigrants Are Stranded In Antwerp Through U.S. Law," New York *Times*, June 17, 1921, p.1.

purposes, the open borders now were closed and would be for forty years.

Even the administration of this restrictive immigration system was unique, and in its limited quotas, clearly biased against people of eastern European origin. The quotas were levied on a monthly basis. As soon as twenty percent of the annual quota for a specific national group was met in a month in all ports of entry combined, no more could be admitted that month in any port. Ships full of hopeful immigrants – in some cases with thousands aboard – streamed across the North Atlantic as fast as they could near the end of each month so that they could land in New York (or Boston) as soon as possible after midnight on the first day of the month and have barges carry the immigrants to Ellis Island for quarantine and processing. Arriving that early in the month was presumed to assure that there was at least twenty percent of the quota still open for those who were "acceptable" immigrants. Ships that arrived in New York on the last day of the month might anchor in Gravesend Bay off Brooklyn to await the witching hour of midnight, marking a new month and a new quota.

Many immigrants arrived in New York in the late nineteenth century with intentions of settling in the Dakotas and Montana to homestead on seized Native American land promised by the U.S. government and/or railroad companies eager to extend population service areas. Those newcomers followed a common trail. From New York City, they could travel by the New York Central Railroad up the Hudson River valley, across the Great Lakes shoreline through Cleveland and Detroit, and after as much as two full days, disembarking in Chicago, the end of that rail line. From Chicago, they could take the Great Northern Railroad through Minneapolis, continuing westward into North Dakota and points west. Even small towns such as Wishek had rail service (as early as 1898), and the competing railroads sought to increase farming activity and the expected profits from shipping grain from those areas to the flour mills of Minneapolis. At the height of immigration in the 1880s and 1890s, among the immigrants came "Volga Germans", who flooded into North Dakota from the Russian Empire. They brought with them the German language and culture that had been preserved in their communities in the empire. Railroads accommodated the influx by creating special "colonist rail cars" with kitchens and pull-down sleeping berths to make the long trips nearly tolerable and relatively cheap for immigrant families. Some rail companies had offices in Europe to promote their services and sell land to those who saw the promise of America. By the time Sigmund got off the *Orbita* in New York, there was a well-trod trail.

Living and working in the Sensburg area of East Prussia had been an opportunity for Sigmund to make contacts in the surrounding ethnic German community, some of whose mem-

The Gaschk Store in Wishek ca. 1923

bers, like Gaschk, had families already in America. The promise of employment in the form of Gaschk's letter made Sigmund's processing through Ellis Island much easier than might have been the case otherwise. The twelve-day trip across the North Atlantic from Hamburg was uneventful, as was the cross-country journey to Wishek, and Sigmund's affiliation with Gaschk was brief. He worked for Gaschk's "Jewelry and Musical Instruments" store for less than two years. By 1925 Sigmund had moved on to Bismarck, North Dakota (and acquired a new name, "S.L. von Loewe-K", a little less eastern

European).[22] The short term of employment was not unlike his experience in his homeland, where like a journeyman of old, he moved on to other opportunities. In the two years working for Gaschk, he came in contact with jewelry wholesaler representatives, traveling salesmen from some of the larger manufacturing jewelers and suppliers such as S.H. Clausin in Minneapolis and Charles Beard in St. Paul. These salesmen often also served as useful sources of employment information throughout the region. They were veritable traveling encyclopedias of current professional news as to who was hiring and who was looking. From the Twin Cities, their sales territories often included several states, as far west as Montana and as far east as Wisconsin, south from the Canadian border to Iowa. Sigmund was developing some industry contacts that could serve him well in his new homeland, and by 1925 he had found employment with Knowles Jewelry in Bismarck, North Dakota, a larger town but north and farther west on the prairie.

Putting down first roots now in his new homeland, if not in a permanent job, Sigmund was eager to share his new life in America with his old friends and family in Poland and Germany and took photos that he brought with him when he returned. Some of them may be revealing of a subtle sense of humor. In one, he is posed sitting on a "Jenny" biplane (a Curtiss JN-4H), a plane type that had been the trainer for pilots German fliers faced in combat during World War I. In another, he sits on the bumper and fender of a 1926 Ricken-backer automobile – the irony is delicious, but there he was, a veteran military pilot triumphantly perched on former enemy

---

[22] This was the last time the middle initial L, for Leo, appears, redundant as it is, with Löwe.

aircraft or the namesakes of their operators.[23]

After working for Knowles for two years, he returned to Poland and Germany in the summer of 1927 to participate in his father's 75th name day celebration. A new passport was issued on May 12, 1927, by the German General Consul in Chicago to "Siegismund v. Loewe Kiedrowski", valid for all countries until May 12, 1932. His profession was "goldsmith", his place of birth Berent, and his current residence Bismarck, North Dakota. The passport was unrestricted. With that pass-

Sigmund's 1927 German Passport

port in the summer of 1927, he returned to visit his family, but not before saying his goodbyes to friends in Bismarck, where he enjoyed a party and a "midnight luncheon" on May 13, which apparently was quite a jolly affair, worthy of the society page of the local newspaper.[24]

Two weeks after his festive departure from Bismarck on May 14, he was back at sea on his way to Europe. Upon his arrival, he traveled to Essen to visit briefly with his brother Johann and family before taking the train to Danzig. Since he was traveling on a German passport, there were no

---

[23] These photos survived only in negatives, suggesting that he took the prints with him, keeping the negatives. Other photos, available as prints, taken in Poland and Germany, are not available as negatives.

[24] The Bismarck *Tribune*, May 14, 1927, p.5.

indications in that document of his arrival in Germany or any subsequent travel. While with his brother in Essen, Sigmund managed to acquire a walking cane, quite the rage with men in the 1920s, especially in Europe. Photos from that visit show him with cane in hand or resting on a bent knee, not unlike the poses his brother took at the time. The *bon vivant* of Bismarck was now no less *au courant* in what the local newspaper would subsequently report as the various "capitals of Europe".

Sigmund arrived in Danzig and cleared Polish customs on June 14, with a visa good for an additional four weeks, until July 14, 1927. A few blocks from the old center city in Danzig he visited the jewelry store of J. Neufeld, *"Uhrmachermeister"* (master watchmaker) at 26 *Goldschmiedegasse* (Goldsmith Alley, now called *Ulica Zlotnikow*). There he purchased five gold pocket watches in what are called hunter cases (with the watch stem at the "3" on the face, not the "12"), with snap-open solid fronts that had to be opened to view the face, which seem to be made for fashion, not convenience, but also protected the crystal from damage. One of the watches was left to be engraved with the initials AVK and picked up later. After buying the watches, he took a train to Tczew, arriving there the same day, visiting Klemens, and the next day he was in Kościerzyna with his parents. He traveled back and forth between his family members, finally departing Tczew on June 30, and obtained a general visa on July 2 in Kościerzyna. From Kościerzyna he traveled to Danzig, arriving there on July 5. Engraving on the one watch completed, he left for Kościerzyna with the watches in their handsome felt-lined boxes from Neufeld. He had left home for the promise of the land of plenty. To him at least it may have seemed appropriate that he would return with gold watches for everyone who had personally and financially helped him emigrate.

Each watch was to be presented to a brother and the engraved one to his father, Anton, the initials AVK for Anton von Kiedrowski. Two of the watches still exist in the family, including the engraved one and the one given to Johann. Since one brother, August, had been killed in World War I, a fifth watch may have been given to brother-in-law Johann Sieracki, husband of Sigmund's sister Maria. The act was an interesting one, perhaps full of meaning for all. Sigmund had left the family home in Poland in 1923 as a journeyman watchmaker, sailing to America on money largely borrowed from family and on a train ticket sent

Watch given to Anton

to him by another immigrant watchmaker living on the plains of North Dakota. He was the youngest in the family, and now he returned with gold watches for everyone. After spending his early career in Germany as a "watchmaker", on the passenger manifest of the *Orbita* on May 23 of 1923, he left Europe for America as a "goldsmith". And that is how he described his profession from that point forward.

As a journeyman watchmaker or goldsmith, Sigmund did not make a lot of money, but what money he made was in U.S. dollars, at a time when German currency had still not regained its prewar level, and a stable Polish currency had just been re-introduced. According to a note in his pocket calendar, the trip from Hamburg to America cost $203.18, plus a tax of $8.15, no small sum for a one-way ticket.[25] In his early years in America, his brother Johann had sent him a few dollars (from $10 to $20) every few months. As slim as his finances might have been, they were still in a currency more stable than the local Polish or German. And he would make an impact.

His decision to make a trip back to the "old country" was occasioned by the celebration of his father's 75th name day and birthday in July. The celebration had been planned for some time, and all the surviving siblings were there. Family lore is that for two days, the five surviving brothers lacked meaningful sobriety and created "havoc" in the town of Kościerzyna, where Anton and Anna still lived. In any case, the saturnalian celebration was something that gave Anton great joy and pride; he talked about it for many years afterward, and his memories were passed down to his grandchildren since it was the last time his five surviving sons were together with him. The town square, doubtless having echoed with similar revelries over the course of its several hundred-year history, once again was the site of a raucous celebration. Like then, for years afterward, whenever the brothers got together with their respective families in Poland, they always managed to get away for evenings to "talk". Anton often chided them over how much talking must have taken place for their wallets to have become "so flat", suggesting that perhaps talk was accompanied by excessive consumption of adult beverages.

In 1927 three of the brothers lived in Poland or Danzig: Anastazy lived in Toruń. Klemens lived in Tczew, also in Poland, close to the border with the Free City of Danzig and East Prussia. Tczew had a small (12.5% according to the 1921 League of Nations survey) German population. Władysław, at the time, lived in the Free City of Danzig, where the majority of the population was ethnic German. Johann lived in Essen, Germany. It was a family occasion with international flavor.

---

[25] Roughly equivalent to $3000 in today's currency.

For the first time in at least four years, the family was together again. It is easy to imagine that they had much to catch up on. It would have been only natural, with a brother visiting from America, that his experiences and observations of that distant and shining land were the subjects of many of those well-lubricated conversations. He had traveled across nearly half the country to a job on the North Dakota steppe. Not only had he gotten a glimpse of New York City, but Chicago as well, and maybe even the Twin Cities of Minneapolis and St. Paul. His train covered more than three times the distance from Danzig to Essen – it was more like Moscow to Paris, a distance none of them had ever traveled. But other family members had stories to tell as well. He had visited Johann on his way to America just months after France and Belgium had occupied the Ruhr area of Germany. It was Johann who scribbled on the back of a photo instructions on how to travel from Danzig into the "occupied territories". Now the French and Belgians were gone after a two-year occupation. Germany had turned the corner with its economy, quickly becoming an industrial powerhouse, but one with political problems in the weak Weimar republic. Yet, now he had something to boast about, certainly in terms of what Sigmund remembered from the spring of 1923. Germany was succeeding in its obsessive drive to recover its greatness and leadership in the growing world community.

Anastazy, Klemens and Władysław also had tales to tell from their experiences in the newly-reconstituted Polish state. Anastazy's career as a national police officer was continuing well, but he was exposed to the inter-ethnic conflicts caused by Poland's expansion into areas to the east and her borders with Germany to the north. Living in Toruń with his wife Zofia, their family had grown to four, with the addition of Maria, born in 1924, and Henryk, born in 1925. The remaining bachelors, Klemens and Władysław, were not yet married, but both had attended a school of business that prepared them to take advantage of the promise of a growing but still stunted Polish economy.

There was a topic of discussion – or perhaps an unspoken awareness – that was likely the most uncomfortable of all on this occasion of celebration. August's ultimate fate was never determined. Reported missing in the lists of November 9, 1918, it was by now certain that he had been killed in the war, but there was no satisfactory closure. He was gone, but there was no documentation as to place, time or cause. He was simply missing in action. No word of being wounded. Not captured. Just unaccounted for. With no proper grieving process, their grief became indefinitely extended for the brother who had been lost in the charnel house of France and Belgium. The loss was ambiguous but no less real and would become a perpetual uncertainty. There were many opportunities for a solemn toast among the revelries.

Whether they carried on their conversations in Kashubian as they had as children, or German, which was probably more comfortable for Johann than Polish would have been, is unknown. For Sigmund, it was a complete respite from having to speak English, but he had gravitated toward German communities in Wishek and Bismarck, so the struggle with English – in which he had never had any formal instruction – was not much of an issue in his new life.

Over the next several weeks, Sigmund made more wallet-flattening social rounds, visiting old friends as well as family, especially in Tczew, Kościerzyna and Danzig. He had stories to tell that everyone was eager to hear. With his variety of travel documents, he was able to cross the many borders in the area without much difficulty or delay. On one of his trips to Danzig, he visited the American Consulate and obtained a non-quota visa (the first for that year) dated July 20, 1927.

By early August, he was back in Essen with Johann and his family. After about two weeks in Germany – most likely the whole time in Essen with his brother Johann, his wife

Leocadia, and their children – on August 22, 1927, Sigmund left Bremen for his return trip on the United States Lines ship the USS *Republic*. With its 1051 passengers, the ship stopped in Southampton, Cherbourg, and Queenstown (now Cobh, Ireland) on its way to the U.S. Sigmund disembarked when it landed in Boston on September 1, and the ship continued, arriving in New York on September 2. His name on the passenger list (Tourist Third Cabin passengers) was "Mr. Sigismund von Loewe-Kiedrowski".

Although the other brothers, their sister and families would get together frequently over the next dozen years of peacetime, waxing nostalgic about Anton's 75th name day celebration and attempting to relive the occasion that they so enjoyed, the brother from America would never return, nor would he ever see his parents, brothers or sister again.

CHAPTER FIVE
The Immigrant

Sigmund left Europe with warm memories and cold job prospects. It had been eleven years since he had completed his apprenticeship with Golembiewski in Putzig and received his certification as a journeyman watchmaker. The war and the following political and social upheavals whiplashed his career path, ultimately driving him to immigrate to America. Now he was faced with finding new employment with a search carried on long-distance from Europe during the three months he had been abroad.

After arriving in Boston on September 1, 1927, Sigmund traveled to Milwaukee. He knew a family there, Alexander & Valeria Prinz and their five daughters. Their middle daughter, Gertrude, was five years younger than Sigmund, but it was her name that was in Sigmund's 1925 address book. The Prinz family had immigrated to America in 1909, coming from the village of Heringshütte (Śledziowa Huta today), just 3 km away from where Sigmund was born. The stay was long-planned, and Sigmund received mail there. Especially important was a letter from C.E. Blanchard, a North Dakota representative of S.H. Clausin Company, a Minneapolis wholesale and manufacturing jeweler. Blanchard had called on the store where Sigmund worked in Bismarck during his sales rounds through the Upper Midwest. While in Europe, Sigmund had sent a postcard to Blanchard, stating that he was looking for work for when he returned. In his letter written while on the road in Fargo, Blanchard wrote that he only knew of a job in Harlowton, Montana, a town of fewer than a thousand people today whose website boasts of being within two hours of "four major Montana cities". After Wishek and Bismarck, ever wider-open spaces of the American prairie had little appeal for Sigmund. Blanchard also suggested getting in touch with James Thompson, who was in charge of the materials department at Clausin in Minneapolis, since he often had inquiries for watchmakers. Blanchard also referred to "Mr. Knowles", who could vouch for Sigmund being "very satisfactory". Sigmund had worked for him from 1925 to his departure for Europe in May 1927. With Thompson's help, by the end of the year, Sigmund had found a job in Minneapolis, working for John S. Allen, Jeweler, located in arguably the grandest and most architecturally striking building in the Twin Cities – the Metropolitan.

———

The Metropolitan Building ca. 1905

In 1890, a Minneapolis real estate speculator, shameless hustler and serial swindler by the name of Louis Menage, of dubious character but substantial wealth, invested well over a million dollars – an enormous sum of money for the time, about $30 million today – in a magnificent building that became known initially as the Northwestern Guaranty Loan Building. In the financial panic of 1893, Northwestern Guaranty went bankrupt, Menage fled the country, and the building was sold, and then in 1905 sold again, this time to the Metropolitan Life Insurance Company. It became known as the Metropolitan Building until what architectural historian Larry Millett called an act of consummate "civic vandalism" in 1962 removed it from the corner of Third Street and Second

Avenue South. This Richardson Romanesque structure of twelve stories was reportedly the tallest building west of the Mississippi at the time it was built – the first "skyscraper". This style of architecture was the big-building idiom of the day. The architects of the first Minneapolis Public Library and the Minneapolis City Hall both adopted that style. The Metropolitan's bottom three stories on all four sides were faced with green New Hampshire granite, and the upper stories in red Lake Superior sandstone. No money was spared by the builder.

It was located at the heart of Minneapolis, but that initially advantageous location would ultimately be its downfall. Close to the Gateway area when built, it was the centerpiece of downtown Minneapolis. All roads seemed to lead to the Metropolitan. It was striking in its reddish hue. A forty-foot tower on its northeast corner provided the best view of Minneapolis, but was closed down after a woman committed suicide by jumping from it. Nevertheless, for more than half a century, the Metropolitan was a signature building in an increasingly prosperous city, the largest in Minnesota.

The Metropolitan Building in its heyday contained more than four hundred offices. One of the most prominent tenants in the 1950s was the architectural firm of Thorshov and Cerny. They would be responsible for designing such projects as the Minneapolis airport and Metropolitan Stadium, the home to the transplanted Washington Senators American League baseball team, which became the Minnesota Twins. Ironic is that Robert Cerny was a strong voice that urged the leveling of the Gateway area – including the Metropolitan.

Its twelve-story atrium measured fifty by eighty feet, and six elevators of elaborate iron work trolled up and down on opposite sides of the open space. There was even a rooftop restaurant for a time. Surrounding the atrium, the floors outside the offices were translucent glass, which brought even more light into the entire building. The first floor was largely service or retail stores, such as a stationer, dry cleaner, barbershop, and soda fountain/lunch counter (eventually, Chatto's "Chat 'n Chew"), as well as a Minnesota Motor Vehicle Bureau branch office. There was also a lunchroom called Nellie's in the basement, operated by Nellie Thomas. In addition to the two main entrances to the building, one on Third Street, and another on the east side on Second Avenue South, there was a third, less grand entrance down a few steps from the parking lot of the U.S. Post Office. When a new post office was finished in 1933, the old became the Federal Courthouse. Just inside this entrance were two small retail "suites". From the parking lot, one could walk up a short pedestrian alley and come out on Fourth Street, right at the Covered Wagon Restaurant, whose popular frontier theme served as an occasional lunch spot for local office workers.

This third, west entrance was unusual in that the revolving doors were about fifteen feet inside the building, with heavy swinging doors serving as the access to outside. This created something of a vestibule flanked by two small shops, one a stationer, the other a jewelry store. In the rigorous Minnesota winter, it also created a very chilly space for those stores that opened onto it.

In 1897 a jeweler by the name of John S. Allen moved into one of those spaces. Four years earlier, when Menage had lost the building and Northwestern Guaranty, the building was sold to another local investor, Thomas Lowry, owner of the streetcar system. Since 1886, when he was twenty-seven, Allen had occupied different spaces for watch and jewelry sales and repair around the downtown area. He moved his store first to a basement space, then to suite 110 in the Guaranty building. For the next sixty years, there would be a thriving jewelry store in that modest space. The jewelry store space rented by Allen measured about 20 x 25 feet. Suite 110 was, by contemporary accounts, at best a modest store space, at worst a hole in the wall. The rent was equally modest and changed little until its demolition in 1961.

Because of the natural incline in the block rising northeast to southwest, the west entrance had several steps down from the parking lot level to reach the first floor. As you walked into the store, you were surrounded by three glass counter cases of watches and jewelry. Larger items were displayed in the wall case like a built-in china closet on the far side of the aisle behind the middle glass case. Beneath the glass wall case were cabinets which, among other things, contained a stone crock of hydrochloric acid solution for cleaning jewelry. Between the counter case on the right and the one straight ahead at an angle was an artfully crafted swinging wooden gate, which allowed access behind the counter cases and to work areas, safe, and wall displays.

Since the store was about three feet below the grade of the parking lot, the store's only exterior window revealed its interior. Curious pedestrians could peer into the store and see the stool and workbench, where watch and jewelry repairs or adjustments could be made. Next to the workbench, secured to the floor, was a foot-operated treadle that powered the jeweler's lathe. A shelf behind the stool area held machinery and jars of solvents – mostly benzene – for watch-cleaning.

Diagonally opposite the workbench, on the right back corner of the store, there was a huge safe whose hulking size (at least five feet tall and three feet across) belied the presumed mobility suggested by the large wheels it rested on. Once the safe was filled with the more valuable contents from exterior and interior cases and was closed for the day, security was provided by a stool which had one leg resting firmly on a nail that passed easily through a hole in the floor, which when removed, closed a switch and sounded an alarm bell powered by dry cell batteries. The system was activated by a knife switch under an exterior showcase to the right side of the door to the store. Once the stool was in place, and that switch was thrown, large cotton dust covers were placed on the counter cases to hide their contents, and the front door was closed and locked for the night. The floors were bare wood, probably without a finish since the building was finished in 1890. Yet, very regularly, a cleaning woman came in with a simple mop and bucket to dutifully slop water around, presumably to clean the floor, but probably doing little more than moving dampened dust into new spaces.

At its peak occupancy in the 1940s and 1950s, the thousand workers in the Met's offices constituted an enviable source of prospective customers who spent their working hours in the building every day. It was convenient – especially during Minnesota winters – to take an elevator down to the main level, grab a bite at the lunch counter, get a haircut, or pick up office supplies on their lunch hour, and without stepping outside, be able to shop the watches and jewelry displayed in the brightly-lit cases. Though tucked away from most of the main floor shops, the store benefitted from the small-town equivalent population that worked in the Met, and many people who worked in the building patronized the jewelry store for purchases and repairs. Government employees from the Main Post Office (the Federal Courthouse after 1933) across the parking lot also found the convenience of the store appealing. The Minneapolis Federal Reserve Building was close by, as were other banks and office buildings, most notably the flour mills of Minneapolis – Pillsbury and General Mills, and the clientele included Twin Cities notables such as the Weyerhaeuser and Pillsbury families.

Sigmund arrived in Minneapolis in 1927 and spent the last thirty years of his life in that store, being its last owner before the Metropolitan Building collapsed under the wrecking ball of government-sponsored philistinism and became a parking lot for nearly twenty years. With all that he had experienced to that point in his life, he might have been tempted to believe he could now settle into a comfortable routine expected for the youngest in the family. Such expectations would prove to be false. Although his personal life would change dramatically, largely for the better, his role in the family would ultimately undergo a tectonic shift. The former status of beneficiary had evaporated, and mostly through his own efforts.

Sigmund's journey from the dusty North Dakota plains town of Wishek to the metropolis of Minneapolis in just five years, with a two-year stopover in Bismarck, was remarkable. Bismarck, with a population of less than eight thousand, was colossal compared to Wishek, which had a population measured in the few hundreds. The society pages of the Bismarck *Tribune* suggest that Sigmund was a figure of note in 1927. His "midnight luncheon" party in May and his return four months later were a source of interest, if only because no one else in Bismarck seemed to be doing it. The Bismarck *Tribune* reported on page 6 of its September 19, 1927 edition: "S. Von Loewe returned from a four-month trip to Europe. Mr. Von Loewe traveled through the principal countries of Europe and visited relatives at different points".

When he settled in Minneapolis, he was now in a city comparable in size to the Free City of Danzig, where friends and relatives lived and worked. The Twin Cities offered many opportunities for new German immigrants to settle into their new country with a minimum of alienation from the old. No longer did he stand out as an unusual traveler or immigrant. Although Minneapolis had nowhere near the percentage of ethnic Germans that Danzig had (reportedly ninety-eight percent), there were social clubs and fraternal organizations that provided opportunities for German immigrants to meet others who wished to preserve their heritage. There were even singing groups of various levels of quality, such as the Liederkranz Singers, which he discovered and happily participated in (but which his future wife sniffed was somewhat amateurish). He even served as an officer in organizations such as The Minneapolis Arion and The Germanistic Society of Minnesota (with his official address, 110 Metropol-

itan Building). Without hesitation, he yielded to the tempta-
tion of preserving his German identity by becoming active in
these fraternal groups. St. Paul as well was a focal point of the
German community, especially with The *Volkszeitung*
Printing and Publishing Company on East Third Street.

Being active in such organizations, however, could have
worked counter to his best interests as a retail businessman.
Although hired as a watchmaker assistant to John S. Allen,
who was then nearly seventy, Sigmund became increasingly
the face of the store to customers. In the modest store space,
there certainly was no room to hide. Some facility with English
was essential; he had to be fluent in order to anticipate and
handle the needs and wants of those who entered the store.
But a tinge of a German accent probably even helped a bit by
providing a cosmopolitan air. Like any good salesman, he was
sensitive to the interests and feelings of clientele. With the
military personnel, he worked hard to puzzle out the
confusing ranks of army and navy. Stripes, stars, and
"scrambled eggs" became second nature to him in just a few
years. Yeomen and captains, admirals and colonels, all found
their way into his store and found themselves addressed by
correct rank and with dignity by this former aviator, whose
military past and affiliation remained unmentioned.

His military experience, now long ago and far away behind
him, combined with his national origins, led to an occasion in
the early 1930s, once reported in a local newspaper, when he
spoke to a Twin Cities German-American club about the future
of air power. What he said specifically is unrecorded, and there
is no longer any indication as to what club it was, but that was
when most of Europe and much of America feared the
bombing of civilians in what many presumed to be the next
war not many years away. One of the horrific innovations of
World War I was that civilian population centers were
targeted for aerial attacks. For members of a fraternal German
heritage club, it was appealing to hear someone of their

national background with military aviation experience speak to a hot topic of the day, one that stirred populations on both sides of the Atlantic.

In the store, not only did his German-tinged English work to his advantage. Almost gangly, he was of medium height, 5' 10" tall, of slight build, and dressed in the suit and tie that were *de rigueur* for most businessmen of that age. Even on picnics or visiting barnstormer friends at airfields, photos show him in a suit and tie. In a moment of informality or sweltering temperatures, he might take off his suit coat. His shoes were always polished, almost to the point of fetish, likely a carryover from his military service. The stiffness of his sartorial appearance was softened by his sense of humor, which bordered on excessively dry but still with a flash of a smile that eventually assured you he was joking. This ability to joke in what was his fourth language revealed a fluency covered by his accent. Some photos suggest that he cut a dashing figure with his coal-black hair and widow's peak, and he made the most of it with the ladies, many of whom he captured (on film at least).

His association with German organizations is intriguing because of the proximity of a large Kashubian population not far away from Minneapolis. Kashubians who left West Prussia in the 1860s and 1870s had settled in the city of Winona, Minnesota, and their community was vibrant and growing. There was a sizable Polish population in Winona as well, not just a few of which were probably ethnic Kashubian originally. Yet, there is no evidence that Sigmund ever reached out to the Kashubs of Minnesota, even though he had been raised speaking the language at home. Clearly, he had broken with that ethnicity in favor of being considered German – which, not incidentally, was the largest ethnic group in Minnesota.

His salary at the store was modest, and that fact made it difficult to find suitable, affordable housing. For his first three years in Minneapolis, he resided at the YMCA on Ninth Street and LaSalle, typical for newly-immigrated single men. Residence at the Y solved not only the problem of cost, but it was an easy walk from his room there to the store in the Metropolitan Building. Of course, given the frequently harsh Minnesota winters, he more than once caught a streetcar on Nicollet Avenue to avoid the weather for those few blocks.

The center city location of the Metropolitan Building with its various services attracted a lot of office workers from surrounding buildings as well as from the Metropolitan itself. One lively, short, brown-haired woman, in particular, a stenographer at Pillsbury Mills, which occupied the entire third floor at the Met, showed considerable interest in the jewelry on display. Sigmund was happy to help her out whenever she came in the store, usually during her lunch hour. Eventually, they were attracted to each other. She had been born in Lake Mills, Iowa, but raised in Fargo, North Dakota. Her name was Marvyl Larson. Although a corporate secretary with consummate shorthand and typing skills, she was also a professional classical singer, a lyric soprano. They had in common a long work history despite their ages. Marvyl was no younger than twenty-eight when they met – although in the 1930 U.S. Census she claimed to be twenty-seven (when she was actually twenty-nine). As early as age nineteen, she had worked as a stenographer at Standard Oil in Fargo after graduating from Fargo High School.

Not exactly a character from an F. Scott Fitzgerald story, in some ways, she was typical of the American "flapper" of the 1920s. She was among those "girls" who left rural settings for the bright lights of the big city as America became increasingly urban. Many of those young women fought for personal independence, equality in pay and a voice in the politics of the day. They became active in sports like golf and tennis, smoked cigarettes (touted then as a healthful habit) and drank alcohol (surreptitiously, of course – Prohibition was in effect). They were often characterized as frivolous and even brainless. A graduate of Concordia Conservatory in North Dakota, Marvyl was definitely a woman ahead of her time in terms of employment and autonomy. And that was a problem – for her parents and, to a different degree, for Sigmund.

Marvyl had attended the American Conservatory of Music in Chicago, where she had also worked as a secretary in Pillsbury offices. She had performed on radio station WGN, even receiving fan mail from as far away as Madison, Wisconsin. However, her mother and father were a bit dismayed by her residence in Chicago, a long way from Fargo, and called her back, arranging for her to stay in Minneapolis (in their view a much safer, but more importantly, closer, city) with her father's sister Gyda Stadhem and her daughter Stella. Stella was seven years older than Marvyl, and was a school teacher in the Minneapolis public school system. Sarah Larson, Marvyl's mother, was much happier with that arrangement than what she had in Chicago, so she worked for Pillsbury in Minneapolis as a secretary, but hadn't yet gotten out of her system her passion for singing on bigger stages than the Upper Midwest.

Sigmund had moved out of the YMCA by the time he received his naturalization papers in January of 1931. He had established himself as an American of German descent; his naturalization papers specified that his "race" was German and his "former nationality" was German. He had put down roots, albeit shallow, living in an apartment out on Hennepin and 27th in south Minneapolis – not far from Temple Israel, where Marvyl was a regular

member of the temple vocal quartet. He was prepared to take the next life-changing step – proposing marriage to Marvyl – when she announced in the summer of 1931 she was going off to New York to follow her vocal career. This was a stunning setback for him. He had lost her to her career, and he was devastated.

Marvyl spent a number of months in New York City. She performed on the radio during November of 1931. Her performance on November 20 was on WABC with Toscha Seidel, the Russian violinist, and the Lester Lanin orchestra. There were other concerts and recitals, but in a short time – much to Sigmund's relief and delight – she returned. Whether motivated by her love for Sigmund or out of respect for her parents' wishes as had been the case in her return from Chicago a few years earlier, is unknown. Five months later, she and Sigmund were married at her sister Viola's home in Fargo in a small family ceremony. What may have passed for a honeymoon in that era of economic troubles, they took a trip out to Bismarck to visit Sigmund's friends before returning to Minneapolis.

Their first child, a daughter whom they named Gretchen, was born in 1934. By that time, the Great Depression was firmly in place. Marvyl continued her singing job at Temple Israel in Minneapolis and gave private lessons two days a week at MacPhail College of Music, but largely stayed home to raise their child. She also kept her hand in singing with the St. Paul Opera Company, and occasional church jobs as well, such as House of Hope Presbyterian Church in St. Paul. Sigmund's employer, John S. Allen, frequently skipped paydays for his only employee, pleading that times were difficult and he needed the money because the Metropolitan was losing tenants and customers as the Depression persisted. Payless paydays became frequent and painful, but in spite of all the economic problems and family financial challenges, Sigmund and Marvyl managed to buy a house for $3400 in south

Minneapolis in early 1935, a three-year-old home on Thirteenth Avenue in the Shenandoah Terrace subdivision, purchased from the estate of the original owner.

In less than a dozen years, Sigmund had gone from Ellis Island immigrant – the youngest in his family with considerable financial help from family – to American citizen, fully employed (if not always paid) jeweler, married to a professional woman with whom he had a child, and owner of his own home. He continued to stay in contact with family members left behind when letter-writing and telegrams were preferred to the exorbitance of trans-Atlantic telephone calls. Visits to his birthplace were simply out of the question. The family had his business address at the Metropolitan, and that is where he received mail for years to come.

He had achieved the American Dream at a time of deepening worldwide economic catastrophe. As the decade wore on, dictators stirred their populations to tribal nativism from the Far East to Europe. By 1939 Sigmund would be a helpless observer as family in Germany and Poland were caught up in the horror. Only one other family member would escape to America in time to avoid suffering, death, or imprisonment.

CHAPTER SIX
Johann, His Family and His Agenda

With Sigmund's emigration from the chaos that was Germany in May of 1923, the family diaspora was complete. They were now spread out on two continents in three different countries: Anastazy, Klemens, Władysław, and Maria in the new Poland, Johann in Germany, and Sigmund in the United States. Each of those countries had been affected by World War I differently, and each would respond to post-war challenges and the Great Depression in its own way and play its own role in the coming and prosecution of World War II.

There would be the quotidian rhythm and routine of life as the brothers who weren't yet married would marry, children would be born, some of those children would have the opportunity to leave their families behind, some would not survive to adulthood, and some would settle into a relatively comfortable existence. But as the world economy collapsed and deranged psychopaths emerged as heads of state in Europe and Asia, what little comfort there was came to a crashing end. Like the proverbial frog in a pot of water being heated on a stove so slowly that the frog feels no need to escape until he is boiled alive, so Europe and the world in general moved slowly and inexorably to the unspeakable horror of a second global conflict, more savage and deadly than the first. Germany was the prime example of economic and political issues driving a country toward dictatorship under the stress of the depression, and its headlong rush away from democracy was only intensified by the desire to recover Germany's former greatness and escape war guilt. But Johann and his family seemed oddly unaffected by Germany's internal turmoil of the 1930s.

As the eldest of the seven children of Anton and Anna, it

was fitting that Johann blazed the emigrant trail for his family, moving to Essen, Germany at the turn of the new century. His was not the customary emigration across national frontiers since he moved within the German Empire. But moving from a small town like Berent to the industrialized metropolitan Essen was no less jarring than moving to another country, though with a familiar language and a large and essentially unfamiliar, not always friendly, population and a faster, urban pace of life.

———

Germany between the wars bore little resemblance to the Germany Johann and Leocadia Lipski knew when they were married. Leocadia was born in 1889 in the small village of Lipa, not far south of Berent. Johann's maternal grandmother Magdalena was born a Lipski, so Johann and Leocadia may have been cousins. Like most women of the time, Leocadia was not educated much beyond the eight years of primary level, and that education was largely aimed to prepare girls for their futures as wives and mothers. The language of commerce and education imposed on them in their childhood was German, not Kashubian. That fact made easier the move to Essen, an area which together with the city of Dortmund, not far away, also attracted Kashubian immigration, but it was clear by her later letters that Leocadia struggled with writing in German.

If any city in Germany was crucial to the war effort of 1914-1918, it was Essen, the industrial heart of the German Empire. It was the home of Krupp AG, the steel and munitions giant. Johann may have been employed by Krupp early in his working life, but by the time of the war, he was already working for the Essen public transit system, joining it by 1911. Essen was dominated by Krupp, and in a sense, even public transit might have been popularly viewed as part of Krupp. Krupp played a significant role in the expansion of the population of Essen, as workers from more rural areas sought employment in the growing metropolis. Its thousands of workers needed transportation to jobs, and as Krupp became the largest company in Europe, Essen became a company town.

There is no evidence that he served in the war – he was the only brother who did not. It may not have been just a reflection of his age (he was 31 when the war started), but possibly because of the importance of transport, even urban trams, to the German war effort. Arms production had been facilitated by a well-developed inter-urban rail system and early in the war made easier the transfer of men and materiel between the western and eastern fronts. As the war continued, staffing and maintaining the trams became increasingly difficult as all able-bodied men were at the front. Non-conscripted officers of the managing company, SEG, and of the city, like Johann, were drafted into positions vacated by the conscripted. They served their country by serving their employers in a different capacity. Eventually, women would fill those positions. The system, with the rapid expansion started in 1911, continued to build up routes and service well into the war years, demonstrating the importance of the city during wartime.

The British blockade of Germany, responsible for the deaths of hundreds of thousands of civilians, was probably felt less in Essen than in other, smaller cities of the Empire because of its favored status as a pivotal player in the war effort. But Johann and his family witnessed the disruption and revolution of the immediate postwar period, the two-year occupation of the Ruhr – including Essen – by the French and Belgian armies, as well as the coinciding crash of the German economy in the early 1920s as hyperinflation spread wildly and broadly. Essen was not immune to the political, social and economic calamities afflicting the rest of the republic. When the German recovery surged in the last years of that decade, it seemed as though Germany's worst years were behind it.

Both Johann's and Leocadia's parents lived in the newly-reconstituted Poland, so what had been an internal – but hardly local – trip to visit family was now complicated by borders that were unfamiliar and delaying. In spite of that, before World War II broke out, there were occasional trips to visit family, usually in August for two or three weeks at a time, with one recorded exception. In the summer of 1931, when Anton and Marianna, Johann's parents, were feted with a 50th wedding anniversary party, neither Johann nor Leocadia was present in the celebratory photo marking the occasion. With that exception, Johann sought to keep in touch with his brothers and sister. Sigmund used Essen and his brother's home as a stop on his voyage to America in 1923, as well as in and out of Germany and Poland in 1927. There were perhaps more convenient routes to Hamburg or Bremen and the trans-Atlantic steamship lines, but none promised more well-lubricated conviviality than the flat on Katzenbruchstrasse.

In 1930, Johann's eldest daughter Hildegard married Hans S, and a year later gave birth to "Hildie Mouse", or "*Mau-eschen*" (little mouse). It was the birth of their first grandchild in late July of 1931 that caused Johann's and Leocadia's absence from the 50th-anniversary celebration of Anton and Anna, Johann's parents.

Hildegard's marriage would be troubled by S's philandering a few years later and his practice of spending the rent money on other things, including a "true love" whom he met while working at a Krupp facility in Attendorn in the summer of 1937. He requested a divorce but was rebuffed, so he expelled Hildegard from the home. Hildegard suffered largely in silence, sharing her travails with her mother and by mail to her elder brother, Hans, but never with her father. S's extramarital activity was brought to the attention of his employer and eventually to state social services, which stepped in. By Christmas of 1938, he and Hildegard were living together again, this time in an apartment in Dortmund, a city which she loathed, calling it dirty, far inferior to Essen.

About the time Hildegard was experiencing her marital difficulties, her sister Irmgard married Hugo F. Irmgard had been an office worker prior to the marriage, but left when she married. She deeply regretted leaving. In her words, it was "mind-numbing boring" for her to stay at home. As she lamented in a letter to her older brother, she missed the office regimen of "two hours' work and one half-hour talk". She knew her former colleagues missed her as well. Although, in her words, her husband was something of a spendthrift, Irmgard was well aware of what Hildegard was experiencing and pledged to herself never to fall into that situation. She was more fortunate in her married life than her sister, but World War II would test her resolve.

Like his younger sister, Hans was of an independent mind with interests, curiosity and ambition that, in his case, eventually took him all over the world. In essence, he became his family's ambassador and their touchstone to other cultures and an uncle who lived in America. Trained as a cook, one of his first jobs was as a baker's assistant at the age of eighteen at a café and bakery in Essen on Steinstrasse. He worked there for a few months and then went on to be a student cook at a restaurant in Bochum until March 1932. For the next three years, he continued his on-the-job training, and by 1935 he was serving on ships such as the brand new "Tannenberg", a passenger and auto ferry that regularly churned the waters of the Baltic connecting the main body of the divided Reich to East Prussia. Even the choppy waters of the Baltic and North Sea apparently didn't satisfy the longing he had for travel, and he soon could no longer resist the siren song of greater seas and exotic ports.

On May 31, 1936, Pentecost Sunday, Hans left his Essen home. Before long, he was serving on various cargo ships that called on ports from the Philippines to Florida, sending the family letters from his various ports of call when he couldn't get home for Christmas or any other family occasions. His last Christmas at home in Germany was 1935. Each year his family hoped that he would return for the holidays, but it would be a quarter-century before he did, and there would be by then many family members lost.

In April 1937, he arrived in Boston as a seaman applying for immigration, having come from Naples by way of Marseilles on the American Export Lines cargo-passenger ship *Excalibur*. The ship's exterior frumpiness belied its elegant even luxurious accommodations for a small contingent of wealthy passengers traveling from the Mediterranean to New York. Following in the fading footsteps of his uncle, Sigmund, by 1938, he had settled down in the United States, practicing his culinary skills in restaurants where the clientele was much more demanding than ravenously hungry and culinarily uncritical merchant sailors.

Correspondence between the family and their ship's cook son was spotty. They were always eager to receive letters from him, but their letters often trailed him in his travels, and their letters that did find him reveal that he was not a very good correspondent while traveling. Occasionally a kindly landlady (with maybe a correspondence-averse son herself) would forward their letters to his next address in the case she knew it, but many letters were returned to his family when he had already moved on from the last address they knew of. Not surprisingly, they were concerned for his fate until he finally wrote them. His mother even speculated maybe only half-jokingly that he disappeared from the water so long ago that even "the sharks had swum away". It was only after he settled in the United States that most of their letters caught up to him regularly, but it was no less difficult for him to get home for even special occasions then, like Christmas or even his younger sister Irmgard's wedding in August of 1937. His last port of call before settling in New York was Miami, which he left in early April 1938. He eventually found his way to Chicago, where he would cook for many years in a local restaurant called Yonkers. His Uncle Sigmund in Minneapolis was his closest relative in the U.S.

Johann and Leocadia and their immediate family had experienced a series of stunning life transitions from Imperial Germany through World War I, revolution and the Weimar Republic with French/Belgian occupation of Essen, and now to Hitler's Third Reich. Potentially not the least onerous of these societal shifts was caused by the Nazi ideology that distinguished between Germans and the rest of the world. There were two categories of the German *"Volk"* or race, as some would have it: the *Volksdeutsche,* those who lived in other countries but were German by ancestry (though not Jewish), and the *Reichsdeutsche*, Germans who lived within the boundaries of Germany. In this sense, though brothers, Sigmund was a *Volksdeutscher* and Johann was a *Reichsdeutscher*. A key to all this was proving one's ancestry, demonstrating the legitimacy of one's ethnic connection and supposed cultural superiority. Genealogy could confirm one's claim to being German of whichever stripe, and it was probably during the war, if not shortly after, that genealogical research became most important to the German middle class in particular.

Since there had been no single entity called Germany before 1871, it was in some ways difficult to prove one's "Germanness." Was someone born in the eighteenth century in the Prussian state of Westphalia really a German? Or a Westphalian? A Prussian? How were they culturally different from one another? What about a family that originated in the Kingdom of Poland in the seventeenth century or earlier? The inconvenient truth was that the Lew Kiedrowski family was not only not of German origins, but Kashubian, Polonized or Germanized as individual or family circumstances required. When Poland was partitioned by Russia, Austria and Prussia in the late eighteenth century, the area of today's northern Poland became West Prussia. And Prussians were Germanic. Or were they? In actuality, the original Prussians (*Prusi*) were Balts, and were converted to Christianity in the thirteenth century, then in part either exterminated or assimilated by the Teutonic Knights who arrogated to themselves the Prusi name. The Knights were supposed to bring the blessings of Christianity to the benighted heathens, genocide not necessarily being the original intent.

Polish and Kashubian noble families – including some of the Lew Kiedrowskis – dutifully swore allegiance to the Prussian Emperor Friedrich Wilhelm II and his son and successor Friedrich Wilhelm III. Suddenly, Polish and

Johann in 1927

Kashubian nobles were "German" nobles, having sworn allegiance to the Prussian crown, thereby preserving their privileges and economic position as nobles. It was a matter of economic self-interest, not ethnic identity or national pride. This somewhat tortured logic of presumed ethnicity by virtue of swearing fealty to the King of Prussia served well many who sought deep, historical "German roots", an inclination that persists to this day in some quarters – most often among those of Polish or Kashubian origins who live abroad.

Many citizens eagerly sought to participate in the campaign to recover German cultural greatness. Genealogists were employed to research and construct the *Ahnentafeln* or family trees in order to prove their deep German roots – and not incidentally, membership in the nobility – usually based upon documents in the imperial office of heraldry (*Heroldsamt*). Johann, though calling himself Johann Stanislaus von Loewe as late as 1912, soon morphed into "Hans", and spent in his words a great deal of money to prove his family's (Lew Kiedrowski, that is) distant German roots back nearly to the "dawn of history". In a letter reputed to be from him to a cousin in 1935, he wrote that he had several copies of the work made for his brothers. No copy of the genealogist's report has survived, however, so it is impossible to determine the origins or validity of that claim.

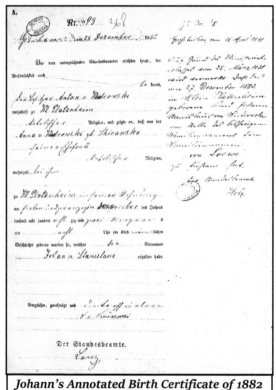

Johann's Annotated Birth Certificate of 1882

What has survived is an unusual annotation on Johann's civil birth certificate from 1882 found in the civil records office in Gross Tuchen. In April of 1931, an official notation was made in the record margin stating that by a ministerial decree (*Ministerialerlass*) of March 25 of that year, the family surname henceforth would be "von Loewe". After years of informally calling the family von Loewe, at the age of forty-eight, Johann changed the family name officially. A surviving official copy of his son Hans' birth certificate dated

June of 1932 also showed the surname as von Loewe, but that copy was issued after the name change that Johann had recorded, reflected in the father's name given as Johann Stanislaus von Loewe.

The notation on a birth record made decades later is occasionally seen in civil birth records. However, in all other cases seen by this author and other researchers in the field, the changes are more orthographic in nature, as modern Polish evolved. For example, a name like O'Toole-Smythe might be orthographically changed to O'Toole-Smith. The change Johann made was more like changing the name to O'Toole. It was a clear change in implied ethnic origins, though one historically valid to a degree. It was not uncommon for the family to be referred to as "von Loewe Kiedrowski" (See Appendix I, "On the Family Name"), but this retroactive pruning resulted in the use of what was essentially a clan name – in a very loose sense – to the exclusion of a toponymic which may have been a better identifier (or betrayer) of ancestral roots. The fact that the name change had ministerial approval suggests that a proper *Ahnentafel* had been created by a genealogist in Johann's employ, and he had submitted it to authorities.

Sigmund chose to be naturalized as an American citizen also with the surname of von Loewe in January 1931 just three months before Johann's birth record change.[26] Von Loewe-Kiedrowskis abroad were now becoming von Loewes. Sigmund had long been using that surname in America, now naturalized with it, and Johann had made the extraordinary effort of having his birth record annotated with the change.

Proving multiple generations of German ancestry was not only central but crucial to political, professional and ultimately

---

[26] Sigmund arrived on the *Orbita* in 1923 as Sigismund Kiedrowski. In his 1925 Declaration of Intention to become a citizen, he was Siegmund von Loewe. In his Petition for Citizenship in 1930 he was Sigmund von Loewe.

personal survival in Nazi Germany. Although Johann was a longtime employee of the Essen transit system, it did him no harm to have this additional proof of deep historical connections to German ethnicity. The results of the genealogical research he commissioned validated his surname change, and in all likelihood, it preceded that change, further legitimizing his claim to being German. That birth record change, coming in 1931 as it did, pre-dates Hitler's rise to power, and was less likely a response to the racial policies of that era than it was to the societal trends of the 1920s as Germans sought to explore and recover their ancestral roots and greatness and prove they belonged to this celebrated tribe. But perhaps more importantly, the genealogical work he commissioned might very well have had a salutary effect on the fate of his family in Poland in the difficult years to come.

When after more than a quarter of a century living on Katzenbruchstrasse, the family, now consisting of just Johann, Leocadia and Heinz (and occasionally Hildegard with her daughter Hildegard) moved to Lehnsgrund 52 in the Margarethenhöhe section of Essen. One of the "garden cities" in Germany, this one largely built with Krupp money and named for the founding mother. Residence there was chiefly for Krupp workers and city officials, in addition to a modest art colony. It was a very desirable place to live. At the time, there were thirty-five apartments available, and seven hundred families applied. As Johann's younger daughter Irmgard pointed out in a letter to her brother Hans, their father was "persistent" and apparently very persuasive in his arguments, and they were able to move there in October 1938. This was the last section of the ambitious project that had been started in 1909. It was without a doubt for that time a very comfortable, spacious and modern two-story flat, in an attractive location, just minutes from Grugapark, even then a lushly wooded public park that had been created a decade earlier. Little Hildegard, age seven, said the new flat was so quiet that you could "hear the fleas jump".

Persistence may indeed have played a role, but perhaps Johann's long tenure in the Essen transit system figured more prominently in the choice by the housing authorities. As in most industrialized countries of that time, public transit had become a critical element in the German economy, especially in the large industrialized cities like Essen. Factory workers had to get to work each day and return home at night. Tram lines, introduced in Essen in 1894, had become vital to the munitions and armament production spewing forth from the Krupp works with its thousands of workers. Having served for more than a quarter-century in this vital service, instead of a tram ride, Johann now had a fifteen-minute walk through the forest and rose gardens to his office. That walk was a real advantage to Johann, who spent long days seated at his manager's desk. His health had deteriorated, and the exercise through Grugapark was viewed by his family as beneficial for his hypertension.

Johann, unfortunately, was not the only family member with medical issues. Heinz, the youngest of the von Loewe children, in February 1937 was diagnosed with juvenile rheumatoid arthritis, and spent eight weeks in the hospital wrapped in cotton wool. For some time he gave up on all sports, even bicycling, but by Christmas of 1938, he was writing that he was a fan of boxing and taking it up himself as a club fighter. He joked that with his long arms he would be able to take on the champion of the world, Joe Louis, seeking to avenge the German Max Schmeling's loss to Louis during their second fight in June. In 1938 Heinz managed to get an apprenticeship in the payroll department at Essen transit. A bit scandalous was that a new desk was ordered for the department and it was assigned to him, the boss's son. He was scheduled to complete his apprenticeship in June of 1939, then become an assistant, then a year in labor service, then into the military. He was already in early military training in late 1938.

Johann's hypertension had led to what seems to have been a mild stroke in July of 1938, and he was able to recuperate at the spas of Bad Kreuznach for two weeks. The wedding of his daughter Irmgard to Hugo in October 1937, though joyous, had put him under a lot of pressure since he paid all expenses of what seemed to have been a lavish celebration. Leocadia wanted to help her daughter Hildegard through the difficult times of her marriage to S, but it was not financially possible. There was no surplus money available, and if Leocadia had mentioned it to Johann, it would have been even more pressure that could have had even more severe health repercussions for him. He may have suspected something, what with his daughter and grandchild moving in with him, Leocadia, and Heinz, but he "never knew the details", as Leocadia wrote. As if that weren't enough, in the fall of that year, Johann fell on his right elbow, and the resultant blood clot had to be removed surgically. All these situations, medical and marital, were described in detail to Hans, living thousands of miles away, unable to help with his family's issues in person. Yet, as soon as he heard of his sister's travails, he wired $25 (98 German marks) to Hildegard to get her through her difficult times. She was stunned by his generosity, but Leocadia cautioned him against being too unselfish, living alone in a foreign country where no one of the family could step up to help him should the occasion arise. Hans would many times demonstrate an unstinting generosity toward family in the most desperate of times that were to come.

Even as Germany spiraled downward into the morass of Nazi totalitarianism, the family often took advantage of the *Kraft durch Freude* (Strength through Joy) travel and leisure program, with trips on the Baltic and to Bavaria. KdF, as it was called, provided a wide variety of affordable activities, such as travel, concerts, plays, and outdoor recreation. Hans' family occasionally wrote that they dreamed of such trips, maybe taking them to America so they could visit him. One of the favorite destinations of the family was Upper Bavaria, in the south of that region bordering on the Alps, and in March of 1939, Irmgard wrote that she and Hugo were planning a three-week trip to Africa for 170 marks. This very popular tourism and recreation program created by the German Labor Front, the national trade union of the National Socialist Party that replaced all others, allowed millions to participate at relatively low cost in activities that they would have been unable to afford otherwise, and was characterized by its mixing of social classes, a primary political objective.

In the letters by family members sent to the world-traveler Hans between August 26, 1937, and June 30, 1939 (the last letter received by Hans before World War II was the end of all communication for seven years), there is a conspicuous absence of any mention of social or political events that we have since come to associate with Hitler's Germany. There was no mention of "Kristallnacht", nor of *Anschluss* with Austria, and only a casual comment by Hildegard to her brother Hans in December about war jitters prior to the Munich Agreement of September 29, 1938, annexing the Sudetenland of Czecho-slovakia. The letters were full of chatty, even gossipy news from family and friends, dinner-table conversation – who had gotten married, where an old friend of Hans' was working, who had moved, etc. This family was either insulated from more troubling events or thought them unworthy of mention to their family member living in America. Bear in mind that these were not rural folk isolated by job or geography. They were a middle-class family of a long-tenured civil servant, a family that had resided in one of the most urban, industrialized areas of Germany for nearly thirty years. Yet to read their letters to Hans, they were still untouched by the madness that was coming to a head, a growing menace that was for them largely eclipsed by their very real and intimate family crises.

From the purported 1935 letter from Johann to his cousin

Kazimir, we learn that Johann had begun his attempt to certify German ancestry before the end of World War I. Those actions were part of an agenda that could protect his family from what would befall non-Germans under the Nazi regime. His investment in an appropriate *Ahnentafel* and his changing of the family surname were critical parts of his strategy to prove the family's German origins, spurious though they were. The tribalism of 1920s Germany was a fact that legitimized his efforts, even more so with the rise of Hitler. But the realization of that project would have consequences beyond his immediate family and the borders of Germany.

CHAPTER SEVEN
The Families in the New Poland

Poland, between the wars, was an underdeveloped agrarian state with a weak infrastructure of railways and highways, and fractured political and societal institutions striving to advance economically. It was led by a government dominated by a strongman dictator who managed to hold together a state of minorities, many of whom chafed under Polish rule and looked outside Poland's borders for support. From the establishment of its final and fixed borders in 1922, Poland was surrounded by states that posed an existential threat that only grew worse in the 1930s.

Younger than Johann by at least a decade, the three surviving brothers in Poland, Anastazy, Klemens and Władysław, were all in their twenties when the First World War ended. Their sister, Maria Sieracki, had just turned thirty, and was married with three children under the age of eight. Brothers and sister alike were now faced with the challenge of forging their own life paths through the tangled landscape of the Second Polish Republic. That landscape was littered with the social and political debris of that war and the half dozen that followed.

The head of state for most of the interwar period until his death in 1935 was Józef Piłsudski. This Vilna[27]-born "Lithuanian of Polish culture", as he described himself, saw a multiethnic Poland desirable, a worthy goal at a time when interethnic conflict was widespread. "Ethnic and cultural variety" within the nation he saw as a well of strength and vitality. His view of Poland was more as a tossed salad with each ingredient keeping its own flavor in the mix, rather than a melting pot dissolving all constituent parts – not so much

---

[27] Today called Vilnius, the capital of Lithuania.

assimilation as integration of complementary ingredients. By contrast, his chief rival for power, Roman Dmowski, the leader of the National Democrats (ND), called for combat against the "alien elements" in their midst and the emigration of all Jews from Poland.

Despite a critical need created by its unenviable geographical location, Poland was still unable to industrialize fast enough in the 1930s to develop a capacity for broad-scale armaments production. Beyond the manufacture of some advanced aircraft in very small numbers, it fell behind Germany and the Soviet Union, its two most trenchant foes. What Poland did exceptionally well was the creation of a military intelligence service, among the best in Europe. There was a tradition of military cryptography going back to the early years of the Second Polish Republic. Recent archival discoveries reveal that the "miracle on the Vistula" that saved Warsaw from Russian conquest (and Europe from the spreading of communism in some views) in August 1920, was due less to divine intervention than the breaking of the Red Army radio codes by the Polish army.[28] And it was Polish mathematicians who, by 1933 with some input from French counterparts, cracked the German "enigma" code and became thereby (too well) aware of Nazi intentions for Europe. Their breakthroughs made possible the code-breaking triumphs attributed almost exclusively to Great Britain at its facility at Bletchley Park. But for Piłsudski the Soviet Union was the main existential threat to Poland.

In addition to new borders, government institutions and currency, Anastazy, Władysław, Klemens and Maria all had to face the reality of a new official language – Polish. Though

---

[28] Nowak, Grzegorz, "Szyfrolamacze", *Polityka*, no. 32 (Warsaw, 2005), pp. 68-70, cited in Anna Cienciala et al., *Katyń: A Crime Without Punishment* (New Haven, Yale University Press, 2007), p. 11.

hardly new to them, for all practical purposes outlawed during their school years in favor of German, Polish became the formal language of Poland almost on the announcement of the armistice. This shifting of linguistic gears could not have been smooth for any of them, but each managed in his or her own way to embrace the change. Not surprisingly, the Kashubian language as well was eclipsed by Polish, and during the 1920s, friction was occasionally observed between the two ethnic groups. Inter-ethnic conflict was not unknown in the new state, with nearly a third of its population of over twenty-one million non-Polish, but Kashubs were not usually differentiated from Poles when calculating minorities in the Second Republic. Borders constructed on the basis of majorities rather than the ethnic identity of a region were the model on which the new Poland was built. In East Prussia and Silesia, plebiscites were organized by the League of Nations to determine by popular vote which state to join – Poland or Germany. The results in both cases were contested, leaving largely Polish populations in East Prussia under German control and Upper Silesia passing to Poland by questionable means.

Anastazy was twenty-six when World War I ended, having served first in the 20th Transport and Supply Battalion in Malbork, then in the 26th Sapper Battalion before being captured. Before the war he had completed an apprenticeship as a pastry chef, but that possible career path fell by the wayside after fighting in the war. He returned to his parents' home in Kościerzyna. Ultimately his thoughts moved toward a career in the Polish National Police, which had been created within the Ministry of Internal Affairs as a centralized federal organization with district offices, rather than local ones. His military experience in the war and the following Russo-Polish War of 1919-1920, as well as facility in German and Polish, made a police career in multi-ethnic Poland seem a natural fit for him. He would distinguish himself for twenty years, achieving the rank of Senior Constable (*Starszy Posterunek*) at the provincial level. But ultimately, it was a career decision that proved fatal.

In February 1920, he began as a military policeman in charge of civilian policing in the former Prussian territory, moving on to the national police on July 1 of that year. As noted above, in 1922, Anastazy and Zofia Majkowski were married in her home village of Lamk, a tiny hamlet; its population probably at least doubled when the wedding guests and family arrived. A photo of the wedding party with Klemens as best man shows some very stern people from both sides of the aisle, almost as though Sigmund had hijacked the festivities sharing his early thoughts of emigration, but was more likely a reflection of posed photography of that era.

After the wedding, Anastazy and Zofia took up residence at 99 *Ulica Parkowowa* in Toruń, the city in which the district police headquarters was located. In April of 1924, their first child, a daughter named Maria, was born, and in June of 1925, their son, Henryk. Several years later, in 1931, a second daughter, Leocadia, was born, but in 1936 she died of pneumonia.

Both Klemens and Władysław were also veterans of the war, Władysław a balloon observer, and Klemens, an infantryman. Władysław appears to have been a prisoner of war captured by the British. The official record is not conclusive since it listed Władysław by his middle name, "Konrad", a name perhaps more familiar and more easily pronounced (and written) by English tongues (and fingers). Confirmation has never been found, but although the birthdate is off by two years, the place of birth, Berent, is correct. The parent name is "Albert" von Kiedrowski. No Albert von Kiedrowski (nor Konrad, for that matter) is recorded in documents of the Catholic church in Berent, so it could be that someone arbitrarily supplied a name to go with Anton's initial "A". This POW was in the 141st (Kulm) Infantry and was captured at Bellecourt, Aisne, France, and because he had a slight head wound, he first passed through the casualty clearing station. On his part, Klemens shared one story from the war, and that was when he ran "like the devil was chasing him" to outrun a gas attack at the Battle of Verdun in the summer of 1916, but he managed to avoid capture or injury.

After the war, Władysław and Klemens graduated together from a school of business and commerce. Klemens was able to use that education to play a role in the slow process of modernization that Poland pursued over the course of the 1920s and 1930s, while Władysław followed in their father's footsteps as a shopkeeper. Klemens' career illustrated the disorder that characterized life in the Europe cobbled together by the diplomats at the Paris Peace Conferences. Klemens partnered in iron and metal fabrication with Adolf Lietz of Danzig. The name "Adolph Lietz" had been associated with the iron business in Danzig since at least 1865. But despite this long presence in Danzig, Lietz seems to have left the city after the war, and by 1923 he had moved his factory to Tczew to a facility at 18 Mickiewicz Street, even though as "Adolph Lietz" he kept a display ad under Danzig in a local business directory. In various directories from the 1920s through 1942, there is both an Adolph and Adolf, and there is little reason to assume they were different individuals. In Sigmund's 1925 address book, the name is spelled with an "f", with Adolf living in Danzig.

Lietz's move is consistent with the reality that before the war, the basic materials for fabricating iron and steel traveled easily within the German Empire using its highly ramified rail east-west rail network. The materials were converted into finished and semi-finished materials and shipped to internal markets by rail or abroad through ports such as Danzig – without crossing a border. But now, despite a customs union with Poland, fabricating iron goods in Danzig may have become too complicated in terms of tariffs and transport across the new borders. Four separate political entities, Poland, Germany, East Prussia and the Free City of Danzig, now occupied the territory once simply the German Empire. By 1929 Klemens had created a company called "Kiedrowski K. i Ska" (K. Kiedrowski and Company) at that address on Mickiewicz. He and Lietz eventually partnered in a firm called "Lietz and Kiedrowski" in the 1930s as the Depression deepened and industrial demand fell.

It was not unusual for ships arriving in Danzig to offload content onto barges that would then be towed to Tczew. In addition to being an important river port on the Vistula, Tczew was on the main east and west rail line between Berlin and Königsberg, East Prussia. Now trains had to cross Poland's western border with Germany and its eastern border with East Prussia in order to make that rail trip. Tczew connected directly via rail and river to Danzig as well, at least physically facilitating the transportation and distribution of their manufactured goods to Germany and as well as within Poland, but again there were those borders of the Free City of Danzig, and Polish manufactured export goods eventually were directed to the new port of Gdynia within Poland, outside Danzig. A tourist destination and small fishing village on the Gulf of Danzig, when Poland became independent and the Free City of Danzig was created, Gdynia became the outlet to the sea for the Polish Corridor, notwithstanding provisions that allowed the Poles to use Danzig. It became a major urban center for Poland by 1926, and by 1929 a north-south rail line for shipping coal from Silesia was completed, facilitating exports.

Klemens and Hannelore Piekarski were married sometime before 1931, when the two of them were seen as a couple at his parents' 50th wedding anniversary celebration. Scraps of information and anecdotes are all we have about Klemens' personal life before 1939. He and Hannelore had no children. What little we know of him conveys a picture of someone with business skills who moved easily between Polish and German communities. But of all the siblings, he was the one who would become known for expressing their Kashubian roots – and would suffer for it.

On Christmas Day 1927, less than four months after the birthday party for Anton, his son Władysław married Klara Popławski. Klara was four years younger than Władysław, who was already thirty-three, both of them a decade older than was the tradition for first marriages. Her father spoke and wrote only German, and although she could speak Polish, she learned to write Polish only after marrying Władysław. Klara's father, Wojciech Popławski, owned what might be called a general store (groceries and household goods) in Warlubie, a town of about two thousand inhabitants. The store also was an inn and living space for the proprietors. The previous owner was Jewish and may well have decided that the drumbeat of anti-Semitism, soft though it was in Poland, compared to Germany, was an indication of what could become policy if Dmowski and the National Democrats had their way. Wojciech turned over the store to Władysław as Klara's dowry, and the newly-married couple moved to Warlubie, where they would reside and raise their two sons, Czesław, born in 1930, and Zbigniew, born in 1933. Warlubie was almost equidistant on a straight line from Toruń (where Anastazy and Zofia lived) and Tczew (where Klemens and Hannelore lived).

Maria, Anton and Anna's only surviving daughter, married Johann Sieracki, a schoolmaster in the village of Skorzewo, in 1910. Her dowry was a brickyard, but there is no evidence that they ever managed it. They lived in that village, a few kilometers from her childhood home in Kościerzyna. With three children – Elzibeta, Jadwiga, and Jan – by the time World War I ended, their fourth child Zygmunt was born in 1925. Like women of her time and place, she played virtually no role outside the home but was the foundation of the family and the glue that kept them together. As a child, with five younger brothers she was likely kept busy. As a mother, she raised four children on a school-master's income. It was a supporting role, if not entirely behind the scenes, confirmed by the lack of information – even photos – about her. One photo we have is of her and daughters Jadwiga and Elzibeta at Christmastime about 1918. In the photo of the celebration of Anton and Anna's 50th wedding an-niversary in 1931, she is seated to her mother's right, senior to her daughters-in-law. When her parents aged, she was largely responsible for their care, and when they died, she was with them.

Elzibeta, Maria, Jadwiga, ca. 1918

These siblings in Poland, in particular, had to this point led their lives and established their families and work lives against what for them was a gauzy background of international political uncertainty and ethnic minority restiveness. For many years Sigmund's wife, Marvyl, related that his family disowned him for not marrying in the Catholic faith. In fact, those who stayed in Poland denied that was ever the case. There were more immediate issues for them, such as food and shelter during the Depression. They were well aware of the multi-ethnicity of the country they lived in, yet probably never looked beyond the borders of their homeland except for contact with their other brothers and sister. But surviving correspondence between the family members abroad is rare and did not reveal an expressed awareness of the building conflict. Personal contact that took place was chiefly annual visits by Johann – often with family – to his brothers, sister, and parents.

Piłsudski and his successors, after his death in 1935, had no doubts about Hitler's or Stalin's intentions for Europe, starting with Danzig and Poland, respectively. To that end, they had attempted to create alliances with the British and French against Germany and the Soviet Union. British authorities, in particular, satisfied with the "peace for our time" of the 1938 Munich agreement with Hitler, ignored the well-founded warnings from the Poles of Nazi plans.

It was Anastazy who immediately felt the implications of Neville Chamberlain's capitulation to Hitler. Cited with medals for his service in the wars of independence and for time of service, Anastazy had been a senior constable since 1928. Against the background of failing diplomacy, in July of 1938 Anastazy's appointment to the personnel department of the district command was superseded less than three months later by promotion to the provincial command on September 22. Coming three days after the Munich agreement giving up the Sudetenland of Czechoslovakia to Hitler, it was no coincidence. Poland was on heightened alert against Germany as a result of Munich and used the opportunity to annex the disputed area of Zaolzie in Czechoslovakia and incorporate nearly 250,000 inhabitants into Poland. The shuffling of national police resources addressed not only the incorporation of additional citizens and increased territory but also preparation for what was becoming the increasingly likely conflict with Germany. It had become clear that France and Britain could just as easily give up Poland to Hitler as they had Czechoslovakia. Nor was Poland's non-aggression pact with the Soviet Union, such as Czechoslovakia had, any guarantee of survival.

Only following the Nazi invasion of Czechoslovakia in

March of 1939 did the British and French publicly agree by treaty to defend Poland if attacked by Germany. However, the British and French agreed in a subsequent secret protocol that they would take defensive measures for themselves rather than rush to Poland's defense if Germany invaded Poland. Poland was to be abandoned.

The non-aggression pact signed between Germany and the Soviet Union on August 31, 1939, also included a secret protocol that provided for the division of Poland between the two parties. Through the summer of 1939, with everyone expecting war, intelligence agencies, especially the German military intelligence agency, the *Abwehr* and its Soviet counterpart, the GRU (*Glavnoe Razvedyvatelnoe Upravlenie*, the Main Intelligence Directorate), scuttled through Poland, establishing and staffing residencies or stations, legal and illegal, and preparing for the inevitable open conflict, creating security, espionage and counterespionage networks.

For those who stayed behind, whether in Germany or Poland, after experiencing the Great War as combatants or civilians, the two decades that followed were a time of career and family responsibilities as spouses, parents, and grand-parents. They strove to succeed in the face of a flu pandemic, political upheaval and economic collapse, struggling as they pursued careers in commerce and civil service. They were only helpless observers, not participants, in the increasing turmoil. Even Johann's family, the one closest to the most troubling developments, seemed oblivious – or at least unaffected – by the turn of events. He watched his elder son, Hans leave behind his troubled homeland, just as he had watched and helped his brother Sigmund follow his dreams to another country.

The events of the summer of 1939 became even more ominous for the families in Poland. Klemens the industrialist, Władysław the shopkeeper, and Anastazy the police officer could not help but hear the shrill threats from Hitler in April as he renounced the non-aggression pact between Germany and Poland, and they could suspect the lives they had successfully struggled to build over the past twenty years were in jeopardy. But they may have believed public statements that Great Britain and France would defend them if Germany attacked, and that belief may have fostered some feelings of optimism. Ultimately though, as the tensions continued to crank up to new levels of fear, the two-decade era was winding down, marking the end of a generation of independent Poland and a Europe without total war.

That August, the month when Johann and his family traditionally traveled to Kościerzyna to visit Anton and Anna and other family members, events turned from omens to brutal reality, and the family in Poland would forever forfeit the career successes, and peaceful family lives they had struggled to build over two decades. What little normalcy they had in their lives was coming to an end. The new shape of reality would stagger them with unprecedented savagery that would be inflicted on tens of millions like them and their families.

The frog had been boiled; there was no escape from the pot.

CHAPTER EIGHT
Invasion, Division, Occupation

The first bombs of the Second World War fell at 4:34 A.M. on September 1, 1939, just a few blocks from the Lietz and Kiedrowski ironworks. Luftwaffe planes from a field 50 km away in East Prussia flew through patchy fog on a mission to destroy the control and connections of explosives placed by Polish sappers to demolish the vital railroad bridge at Tczew. If Klemens slept through the screaming dive-sirens of the Stuka bombers and the bomb blasts, he probably didn't an hour and a half later when the demolition engineers repaired damaged cables and successfully blew sections of the bridge, rendering it impassable. This was just the first of three strikes the German forces made in Poland before dawn that morning. Two more followed minutes later: Wieluń, where one thousand three hundred civilians were killed while still in their beds, and Westerplatte, where a small Polish garrison was bombarded from the antiquated battleship Schleswig-Holstein, and ground forces from nearby Danzig attacked from land.

Over the next three weeks, German forces poured into Poland from the west, the southwest and the north, forcing the Warsaw government and general staff to withdraw to the Romanian border, hoping there to consolidate and re-configure forces to counter the German invasion. But it quickly became clear that they would have to cross the border and seek a safe harbor because of overwhelming military pressure. Still a somewhat friendly neighbor (though eager to preserve goodwill with Germany), Romania would serve for a short time as a waystation to France, where the government planned to marshal forces to re-take Poland with allied help, or at least form a government in exile.

Soviet troops entered Poland on September 17, and in the

spirit of the non-aggression pact and secret protocols, the Red Army had orders to avoid conflict with any German troops they might encounter. At the same time Polish units, unaware of the secret protocols of the Nazi-Soviet non-aggression treaty, were told not to engage Soviet troops, whose real presence was not always understood – ally or invader? Their role became clear as Soviet forces began their occupation of eastern Poland.

The invading German forces sought to capture as many police and government officials as possible to facilitate the upcoming occupation by identifying and crushing any potential opposition groups. Special units were attached to the regular army to seize police, military and government documents. Faced with what had become an unstoppable German attack, Anastazy, a month before his 47th birthday and a senior administrator with the provincial command of the Polish National Police in Toruń, was swept up in the nation's response to the invasion. As Poland's defenses inflicted heavy casualties on the invaders, eventually crumbling in the face of superior manpower and weaponry, his commander ordered him to take police personnel records and other unspecified critical documents to Romania, where he would join the Polish Ministry of Internal Affairs in exile. He was to turn over the documents to the ministry, which would then find its way to France to assist in forming a Polish government in exile. Anastazy was assigned a car and driver, and with barely a goodbye to his wife and their two teenage children, he and his driver headed southeast the more than 800 km for refuge in Romania and anticipated exile in France.

———

As soon as active warfare between Germans and Poles came to an end, an occupation authority was quickly put in place after a short period of military administration secured the conquered areas. On October 8, 1939, the western areas were annexed to the Reich as separate *Reichsgaue* (state admini- strative districts), *Reichsgau Danzig-Westpreussen* now bor- dering East Prussia, and *Reichsgau Wartheland*, collectively called the *Eingegliederte Ostgebiete* (Incorporated Eastern Territories). The area south of Warsaw and east beyond the Vistula became the *Generalgouvernement* (General Govern- ment), essentially under permanent military occupation. Hitler planned to remove Poles to concentration camps or to the General Government area around Warsaw. The General Government was to be a reserve of low-grade Polish labor for the immediate future, but totally Germanized (or extermi- nated) eventually, essentially one large slave labor camp.

Poland became the first instance of Nazi occupation on a large scale, and although a formal plan would not be promulgated by Himmler until 1941, much of what would become known as the *Deutsche Volksliste* (a list of all Germans) was already being applied in Poland. Those Poles who had been actively involved in national movements or political parties (or the Catholic Church for that matter) could be removed to the General Government, but others with similar failings could be sent to concentration camps in either the Government or the *Altreich* (the pre-Anschluss Germany of 1938 borders, exclusive of the new *Reichsgaue*). Deter- mining who had promise and who had none took time to put in place. Some decisions were easy from the Nazi standpoint: Jews had no rights. Poles with no German blood also were considered subhuman and designated for slave labor and elimination. Polonized Germans were to be settled in the *Altreich* to refresh their lapsed cultural memory. But there were many shades of gray, and in January of 1940, the Academy of German Law prepared a secret report on plans for the mass population transfer of elements deemed undesirable. By the spring of 1940, basic strategy was well established and active, but resettlement policy continued to evolve over the next two years.

The impact of the invasion was neither as immediate nor dramatic for Władysław's family as it had been for Anastazy and his. Despite the multi-front invasion and the Nazis' primary focus on exterminating the Poles as well as the Jewish population, which amounted to nearly three million in Poland, the early extermination efforts were directed more toward Poles than Jews. But because Warlubie was hardly a tempting target of commerce and industry or a hotbed of resistance, and consequently probably suffered little from direct military attack, it took six months for the tentacles of Nazi occupation to reach into their home. In early April 1940, Władysław and Klara were arrested by the Gestapo. That same month Johann made a trip to the *Reichsgau Danzig* and arranged for the placement of their sons Czesław and Zbigniew in homes where they could be properly Germanized. Czesław, age nine, was placed with the family of his mother's older sister, Konstancja and her husband, Franz (Franciszek) Heier, who lived in Grudziądz with their two sons, but not before he was told to learn German, or he would "join his parents in the camps". Franciszek spoke no Polish, but Konstancja spoke both Polish and German. Seven-year-old Zbigniew was placed with his father's brother, Klemens, and his wife, Hannelore, in Tczew. On April 17, 1940, Władysław, was assigned number 022447 and admitted to Sachsenhausen, a camp located in Oranienburg, northwest of Berlin, a day after Klara was admitted to Ravensbrück some 50 km north of Sachsenhausen and assigned the number 3149.[29]

Sachsenhausen was created in 1936 to house the Nazis'

---

[29] Klara was assigned a compound number like the alphabetically first seven inmates brought in on that day. In the intake list she is the seventh, with the number 3149/2537. The first number is in sequence for Ravensbrück, the second cannot be explained. The other six women's second numbers are not in sequence for anything, nor are there any duplicates.

political opponents. In 1938 a large brick manufacturing plant was constructed by the SS on the Oder-Havel canal, not far from the camp at another industrial slave labor facility called Neuengamme. It was in the brickworks that Władysław worked during his confinement. Władysław was just one of thousands of Poles who were sent to various camps in the occupied areas or in Germany, often as "prisoners in protective custody". Existing intake documents from the camp do not specify what his status was – political, asocial, or criminal, the three most common non-racial statuses. In 1940, Poles made up the largest single prisoner group in the camp. Often thought of as only a forced labor camp, seven months after Władysław's imprisonment, thirty-three Polish prisoners were executed by the SS, and in autumn 1941, ten thousand Soviet prisoners of war were executed. Ultimately, thirty thousand inmates would die from various causes. Intervention by his brother, Johann, is usually cited by the family as responsible for Władysław's survival in a camp where thousands perished.

The camp at Ravensbrück was created to hold women exclusively and opened in the spring of 1939 as a penal colony. The village of Ravensbrück was a suburb of the town of Fürstenberg, the train station for the camp. The camp's appearance was unlike the camps that were to hold only men. There were no guard towers, no machinegun emplacements, just a nineteen-foot masonry wall topped by electrified wire. The first view that incoming prisoners saw, whether on the march or on the train (if they had any view at all), was of a forest with the spire of the Fürstenberg evangelical church rising out of the woods, with three lakes around the camp. Like Sachsenhausen, six months into the war Ravensbrück held more Poles than any other nationality.

At a time when Jews and Poles alike were being rounded up and randomly shot or sent to camps to be executed, the treatment of Władysław and Klara may seem mild by comparison. Yet, they were deprived of their freedom and their children and performed slave labor under debilitating conditions for years. Within the family, it is believed that their treatment was mitigated by Johann's intervention. Central to that belief is the story that Johann was friends with Heinrich Himmler and that the friendship made it possible for Johann to help his brother Władysław and Klara avoid worse treatment for a longer period. It is not supported by any historical evidence but is well-fixed in the family's memory. It was common knowledge at that time that during a visit to a camp Himmler for an unexplained reason, might release a prisoner or a group of prisoners. Knowing someone important, whether on a national scale or local, camp scale, was frequently the reason some people avoided harsher treatment or obtained early release. Having the ear of the camp commandant, guard or kapo, for that matter, could lighten the assignments of an inmate. Prisoners who were entrusted by the administration with the assignment of work duties, kapos often were responsible for punishment and even life-and-death matters of their fellow prisoners.

Rules were often subject to change at the whim of an individual and could lead to early freedom – or instant death. But Johann's role in Władysław's and Klara's fates was perhaps less related to an acquaintanceship with Himmler than with something Johann had done years earlier.

In the purported letter (noted in Chapter Six, "Johann, His Family and His Agenda") to his cousin Kazimir in 1935, he had written about the deep German roots his family had. His research, he wrote, had cost a great deal of money and had taken a long time to complete, but it was categorical "proof" that the family was German. Since the final report compiled by the genealogist was distributed to his brothers as well, the document could have been used by Władysław on his own behalf or as intercession by Johann, or even by Klemens for his brother, and may have affected the intensity or term of slave labor that Władysław and Klara were subjected to. Their experiences may also have been determined by the fact that they lived in a region that was incorporated into the Reich, rather than in occupied Poland of the General Government. Their imprisonment in camps on Reich soil may have been in part determined by where they lived, and their term and subsequent release determined by genealogical work commissioned by Johann. Ethnic Poles, whether in the annexed areas or the General Government, by Nazi racial policy were subject to extermination, but Władysław and Klara were treated more as internal German political dissidents.

The deportation of Władysław and Klara and the assignment of their sons to foster homes illustrate the occupation and population transfer policies and their application within the framework of Nazi racial theory. By ancestry, Klemens was no more German than Władysław. Both were graduates of a business school in Poland after World War I; Klemens was an industrialist, and Władysław a retail merchant. However, Klemens and his ethnic German wife were given care of the young Zbigniew while his parents were sent off to the concentration camps. It is believed in the family today that Klara was involved in a Polish nationalist women's group, which may have qualified her for detention and rehabilitation, if not execution. Nothing further is known about her participation or the group she belonged to. She was identified on intake at Ravensbrück as a political prisoner. Władysław's reputation, however, seems to have had no such blemish. Both were apparently considered to be dissidents with sufficiently German roots not to warrant execution. Nevertheless, both were sent off to camps for re-education, and their sons were given an opportunity to become thoroughly Germanized.

Since Klara was admitted to Ravensbrück as a political, a dissident, but the Sachsenhausen intake form for Władysław lacks any indication for any of the prisoners, it seems that they were victims of a common Nazi policy, i.e., to arrest both husband and wife even when just one was considered the dissident. In this case, Klara may have been the target and Władysław collateral damage.

When German troops overran Poland in September 1939, and then the Soviets followed from the east on September 17, there was almost immediate resistance from the Poles. That resistance was unique in what would become Nazi-occupied Europe. In the face of a very violent occupation, the resistance was extremely diverse with little cohesion or coordination. Instead, in the earliest days, there was a multitude of smaller groups, often along the lines of the pre-invasion political parties, each with its own characteristics of membership, but all sharing the goal of removing the occupiers. In addition, the casualties of young men were astounding both in the city of Warsaw and the front lines – over one hundred thousand in those two locales alone. Over six hundred thousand were prisoners of war either in Germany or the Soviet Union. Consequently, the partisan movement was one organized by older men, but expanded by members of the Jewish community and a great number of women. Whether Klara participated in the resistance or not is uncertain, but she alone was identified as the "political" of the couple, and her activity may have been the cause for the separation of the family. Over the course of her and Władysław's imprisonment, their sons were subjected to Germanization as practiced by the occupiers. The Nazi definition of Germanization went far beyond learning to speak German. The intent was to obliterate all traces of the subject's native culture, and replace it with the culture of (Nazi) Germany. Czesław's foster family seemed to meet the criteria of the Nazi occupiers with a family head who knew no Polish, only German. Zbigniew was sent off to Klemens and his wife Hannelore, both of whom knew both languages. What may have affected the boys' living arrangements was that their parents, Władysław and Klara, and all the foster parents, Klemens and Hannelore, as well as Franz and Konstancja, lived within the borders of the Reich, in the province of *Reichsgau Danzig*. That region of Poland was annexed to Germany, unlike the General Government, an area with a pre-war population more Polish and Jewish than the *Reichsgau*. Another factor perhaps coloring the Nazi decision was that while neither Władysław nor Klara apparently avowed any German ethnicity (beyond Klara having a father who spoke only German), one spouse in each of the foster couples could – Franz for Czesław and Hannelore for Zbigniew.

———

Klemens seems to have experienced the invasion very differently, if very early on that sudden Friday morning. Living in Tczew under the occupation, as part of the Reich and now called by its German name Dirschau, he suffered economically, but never really physically, at least initially. Dirschau had become a center of German culture (minority though it was) in the Second Polish Republic. A massive rail hub, it was good business for Lietz and Kiedrowski to locate there for its connection to both German and Polish markets – especially with its close proximity to East Prussia. For decades its railway bridges over the Vistula were a vital connection between Berlin and Königsberg, East Prussia, and manufacturing sought to locate there since its transportation network afforded wide distribution of goods. For that reason, the preservation of the city's rail bridges across the Vistula became an early objective in the invasion.

With the integration of Dirschau into Nazi Germany, the Lietz and Kiedrowski ironworks underwent radical ownership change. Most notable was that the name Kiedrowski disappeared from the company sign and ownership, and Klemens was relegated to being an employee. Yet, his connections with things German, possibly including his partner from Danzig of apparent German ethnicity, may have made it possible for him to assist his brother Władysław and his wife Klara in the fostering of their children. The degree of Germanization that Klemens manifested (via his wife and possibly the Lietz partnership) allowed Nazi authorities to look past his Polish nationality and allow him to take responsibility for the young Zbigniew, providing him with support for learning the German language and culture. Again, Johann's effort to prove the family's German roots in the distant past may have paved the way for the survival of not only Władysław and Klara but of their sons as well. Klemens and Hannelore never had any children, yet they would embrace Zbigniew and his brother Czesław as well, virtually as their own for years to come. Had Johann not commissioned the genealogical work so many years before, it is conceivable that Władysław and his family would not have survived.

The siblings who remained in Europe, whether free or imprisoned, essentially lived out the war within the borders of the Reich, whether the *Altreich* or the *Reichsgau Danzig*. Consequently, they could communicate with each other by mail, though with little expectation of privacy by the decree following the Reichstag fire in 1933 (*Reichstagsbrandverordnung*), even for those not in the camps. But their knowledge of the progress of the war was colored by Nazi propaganda untainted by contrary views from abroad or heavily censored mail from soldiers.

By the middle of 1940, all the brothers, together with their sister in Europe, were in the situations that would persist without significant change for more than two years: Anastazy absent, with no word after he left with his driver for Romania and exile in France; Władysław in a concentration camp; Klemens free, but deprived of his property yet fostering one of Władysław's sons; and Johann living free in Nazi Germany but subject to social and political restrictions, not to mention the constant threat of aerial bombardment which forced his daughters and grandchildren to find refuge far away from Essen. With no information to the contrary, Maria and her husband likely remained in the village of Skorzewo.

Thousands of miles and an ocean away, Sigmund had no way of knowing how what he read in the newspapers or heard on the radio was affecting his family. Johann's son Hans, living in Chicago, also lacked any information about the family for the duration of the war, but he and uncle Sigmund were at least able to be in touch and commiserate. Hans' mother would write in July of 1946 that they had received no letters from him for seven years until his of May 16 of that year. It is likely that reflected more the restrictions imposed by Nazi Germany's censorship or embargo of international civilian mail than Hans' letter-writing habits (although she claimed that she had friends who had already received mail from abroad).

Not only could Sigmund not know what was happening to his relatives in the war, neither could he share with them his own news. In April of 1941, he and Marvyl welcomed a son, Karl, to the family, making the house on Thirteenth Avenue just a bit more crowded and definitely less tranquil. Then the death in September of 1941 of John S. Allen, his employer for the last thirteen years, made it possible for Sigmund to succeed to the ownership of the store that would now be called "VON LOEWE, JEWELER". Letterhead for the store formalized for the public what his friends had called him for years. "Von", never used his given name of Sigmund, apparently a bit more foreign than Von. It was also a bit more acceptable to have a surname of "Loewe" than "von Loewe" at a time of war with Germany. Friends called the couple Marvyl and Von, and for reasons never explained, Von called Marvyl "Skip".

After June of 1940, the war in Europe evolved into a stage of consolidation of brutal Nazi oppression and occupation of most of Europe, with eastern Poland and the Baltic States occupied by the Soviet Union. Even after the invasion by the Soviet Union, there was little apparent change in the European families' lives, except for Johann's household, who now, as invaders and occupiers, experienced another transition in their lives. The families were further separated as the husbands served far away, and their wives and children were shipped off to areas more distant from the increasing allied bombing. The most directly affected was Hugo F, Johann's son-in-law, Irmgard's husband, who would spend most of the war on the eastern front. Hans S, Johann's other son-in-law, the husband of Hildegard, managed to avoid all but four weeks on the eastern front, instead serving in a military hospital office in Garmisch-Partenkirchen, or in occupied France. In a letter some years later, he would contrast the German occupation of France with what he regarded as the allies' inefficient occupation of the defeated Germany. He boasted that in France under Nazi control, there was no shortage of collar studs or cabbages, and "everywhere you looked, order prevailed".

It was on the eastern front that the same Axis armies that had staggered the Soviet Union initially in June of 1941, with a massive invasion force of four million troops, began to show signs of attrition late in that year. Extended supply lines and hostile environment, human and climatic, slowly took a toll on the invaders, and casualties mounted into the hundreds of thousands.

By 1943, the fifth year of the war, the cruel predictability of oppression, labor camps and the systematic annihilation of the European Jews was a commonplace reality of public life. The General Government became the principal site of the

Nazi's implementation of the Final Solution. In the Reich itself, the reliability of the hitherto indomitable German military machine with only moderate privation on the home front, would come to an end for the families in Europe. The rationing of food in Nazi Germany had been largely absent from 1939 until the invasion of the Soviet Union. Slave labor in occupied countries working the farms, and the intentional starving of the occupants of those countries, not to mention those in concentration camps, made it possible to feed the population of Germany easily and cheaply, essentially insulating the home front from the experience of total war at least for a short time.

Growing underground opposition, together with military reversals for the Nazis, began to set the stage for the entire continent's eventual plunge into a savagery not experienced in centuries. And it was on the eastern front less than two years after the initial invasion that what had become gradual attrition became a sudden seismic shift, a shift that not only would change the dynamic of the war and consequently define the fate of Europe for the next half-century, but one that would once again stagger the family.

CHAPTER NINE
Hope and Shock

At 4:00 A.M. local time on February 2, 1943, the vaunted German Sixth Army of two hundred and eighty-five thousand German, Hungarian, Romanian, and Italian troops ceased to exist. With that army's complete surrender, the Battle of Stalingrad was over, with nearly two million civilian and military casualties in the five-month battle. Of the hundred thousand German soldiers who surrendered to the Red Army, only six thousand ultimately found their way home, the rest dying on forced marches or vanishing forever into POW and labor camps in the Soviet gulag.

At that hour, the family at 4705 Thirteenth Avenue in Minneapolis had finished dinner, and Sigmund and Marvyl were following their routine of clearing the table and washing dishes after dinner in the breakfast nook, cleaning up the kitchen, and entertaining their toddler and nine-year-old until bedtime. As soon as the youngsters were off to bed, Sigmund could finish up some watch or jewelry repairs until 10:00 P.M., when he turned on the radio to WCCO and listened to Cedric Adams's familiar voice reporting the local and world news. When the newscast was finished, the lights at 4705 would wink off until morning, like those in most of Upper Midwest homes at that time – as pilots reported – leaving that region in darkness. It would be the next day before Sigmund could buy a newspaper and read a small story reporting the end of the Battle of Stalingrad, the bloodiest battle in history. It was almost a non-event for American media. The public had more interest in the theaters of war where American troops were fighting – North Africa and the Pacific – than somewhere in the unfamiliar recesses of the Soviet Union.

Sigmund had not heard from his family in Europe since the war had begun more than three years before. Listening to

Cedric may have given him some sense of what his brothers and sister and their families in Europe were experiencing, but there was no way for him to know their situations; he could only feel dread, and for good reason.

Sigmund knew family members in Europe were in jeopardy, but there was a worry even closer to home, affecting Marvyl, a concern that came from a not entirely unlikely quarter. Marvyl, for more than a decade, had been a member of the vocal quartet at Temple Israel in Minneapolis. As the persecution of Jews in Germany and the occupied areas became widely known, some members of the congregation, the largest synagogue in the Twin Cities and one of the largest in America, called for Marvyl to be released because of her German surname. Rabbi Albert Minda, spiritual leader of the temple since 1922 and a well-respected community leader, refused to fire her, stating that to do so would have made the congregation no better than those who were persecuting Jews. Marvyl stayed.

———

The magnitude of the defeat at Stalingrad is clear by the unheard-of three-day period of mourning proclaimed throughout Germany by the regime: no radio broadcasts but funereal music, and theaters and restaurants shut down. Little more than two weeks later, the Minister of Propaganda Joseph Goebbels would invoke it in his action calls to carefully-selected fawning fanatics at Berlin's *Sportspalast* indoor arena, calling for total mobilization of the German nation in response to the "blow of fate at Stalingrad" suffered on that date.

In Essen, like most inhabitants of this city spared air raid sirens and bombing for the last several months, Johann and Leocadia had a chance to sleep peacefully through the night, with their daughters and grandchildren safely evacuated to the south in rural Bavaria, well beyond the interest of Allied bombing. A month later, they would experience the worst aerial attacks of the war to that date, attacks that would often continue day and night for five months – but for now it was still quiet under the usual suffocating blanket of industrial haze covering Essen this early morning.

In the forced labor camps throughout Nazi-occupied Europe, the normal day began with reveille over loudspeakers and roll call, early and brutal, and on a February day like this, cold. More than 2000 km away, a massive disruption in the Nazi prosecution of the war had already taken place in the winter darkness hours before camp reveille.

Stalingrad marked a turning point in the war, as the endlessly rising curve of German victories first flattened, then started to decline. Until then, German forces had experienced few defeats, and those were inconsequential in size or significance, with perhaps the sole exception of their failure to take Moscow. From February 1943 onward, victories for the Wehrmacht would be rare.

Although the winter of 1943 was a tipping point in the Nazi subjugation of Europe, the change was likely almost imperceptible to Sigmund's family still under Nazi occupation or imprisonment. As pivotal as the event was, Władysław in Sachsenhausen and Klara in Ravensbrück may not have learned of it right away. Life in the camps was no less soul-crushing now than it had been before Stalingrad. Life outside the camps, in the Reich, was significantly better, but only for those who were not Jews, nor Poles with no trace of German ancestry. Those two groups were being murdered in staggering numbers. There were few Jews left in the Danzig-West Prussia territory, but those remaining and Poles were subjects of constant Nazi terror. The lucky ones were sent to the General Government area as forced laborers, the others were gathered on rail station selection platforms and sent from there to the death camps.

For the preceding year or so in the inner governing circles of the Reich, it was believed and even spoken that the war *could* still be won. Goebbels's speech in February 1943 made it clear that now the war *had* to be won; Germany's very existence depended on victory.

———

The year 1943 was central not only for the future of the war, and consequently, the future of Poland and eastern Europe, but for a discovery that would stagger the family. In the spring of 1943, the German government announced it had found the remains of thousands of Polish officers buried in Katyń Forest, near Smolensk in the Soviet Union, an area occupied by the Nazis since the fall of 1941. An investigation conducted by the International Red Cross determined that the executions had been conducted by Soviet authorities. The Soviets pursued their own investigation with fabricated evidence and asserted that the Germans had murdered the victims. Although imprisonment and executions took place at several other sites, the whole program is referred to most often as the Katyń Forest Massacre.

Anastazy was just one of fourteen thousand five hundred Polish police and military officers captured by the Red Army. He and his driver had been taken prisoner before they could cross the Cheremosh River at Kuty and enter Romania on their way to anticipated exile in France. In addition, seven thousand three hundred other Polish prisoners were arrested by Stalin's NKVD (*Narodnyi Komissariat Vnutrennykh Del* – Peoples' Commissariat for Internal Affairs – the secret police and civilian intelligence service). This group of nearly twenty-two thousand included military and police officers, professors, government employees, and politicians. The prisoners were kept at several different camps, including those at Ostashkov, Kozelsk, and Starobelsk. Immediately upon capture, Polish prisoners-of-war were turned over by the Red Army to the NKVD, which was more experienced in administering prison camps. Anastazy, along with other police and gendarmes, was moved to Ostashkov. This camp, like the other two, was housed in a former monastery. Virtually all prisoners were arrested as "enemies of the people", for they had "struggled against the revolutionary movement" or "against the working class".

The captives were interrogated as soon as they arrived in late September and October, but from November to January 1940, more intensive interrogations were conducted by NKVD officers sent from Moscow to the three camps. All prisoners were deemed "irremediably hostile" to the Soviet Union. Among those prisoners was what has been called the Polish elite, the people who could make up future Polish governments and preserve Polish culture. Stalin would order their elimination and thereby clear the way for the creation of a future colony of the Soviet Union managed by his preferred pro-Communist figures.

Initially, the prisoners were not allowed to have any contact with their families. This policy was changed after about a month when they were allowed to send postcards and letters to their families. This policy continued until March of 1940 when it was suddenly stopped. From late November 1939 until March of 1940, when the executions began, the prisoners were permitted to inform their families where they were being held in the USSR. Their situation and locations became widely known, not only to relatives but to the Germans (still allies of the Soviets) and the Polish government in exile, at that time still in France. Their ultimate fate, however, became a secret that was not discovered for three years and culpability for which was denied by the Soviets for decades.

On March 15, 1940, the Central Committee of the All-Union Communist Party recommended to Stalin that the NKVD execute all Polish prisoners. Stalin and the Politburo (the policy-making committee of the Communist Party) approved the recommendation. The Ostashkov prisoners were sent by rail about 165 km to the NKVD facility at Kalinin (since 1990 called Tver). Upon arrival, they were rounded up into groups of two hundred and fifty with thirty NKVD men handling the process. The number two hundred and fifty was the maximum number of prisoners that could be shot in a night – and all executions were done at night. It was reported by a bystander that two men would hold the prisoner's arms, and a third would shoot him in the base of the skull. At the village of Mednoe, bulldozers were used to excavate enormous pits into which the bodies were tossed after being loaded on trucks at the execution site and driven there. It is believed that Anastazy was in the group that was executed on April 5, 1940.[30]

If Anastazy's wife Zofia received correspondence during his imprisonment, it has been lost. What exactly she knew about his situation and when she knew it has been clouded by time and a pro-Soviet regime that covered up the truth about Katyń for more than half a century. She passed down to her daughter Maria a remarkable story, but one that raises questions that will probably never be answered. It may be a recollection of correspondence she received from Anastazy combined with a report the driver made to her. That story was passed on by Maria to her children just before she died in 1993, fifty-three years after Anastazy's murder.

Shortly after the Soviet invasion started on September 17, 1939, Anastazy and his driver were stopped and arrested by Soviet troops before they could cross the border into Romania. Soviet commanders had been instructed to treat Germans as allies and Polish troops and police as enemies of the people, subject to arrest and confinement. Polish troops, for their part,

---

[30] Anastazy was on the NKVD death list 012/1 for Ostashkov.

had been instructed to not confront Soviet troops unless provoked, in the early stages uncertain as to whether they were allies or enemies.

After arrest, Anastazy and his driver were marched to a railhead in the Soviet Union, where they were loaded into overcrowded and unsanitary railcars, reaching Ostashkov probably in October. No accurate timeline exists for the period from Anastazy's arrest to his likely execution in April 1940. We know that prisoners were moved to the various prison camps in October. In December, the last of the Polish army officers not yet captured were rounded up and sent to one of the three camps. Soldiers of the rank of private and non-commissioned officers were released from the camps and turned over to the Germans as POWs. The driver would have been released at that time, four months before the mass executions started in March 1940 and just a month or so after captives were allowed to write to their families.

Zofia told her daughter that the driver informed her that since his wife was German, she was able to secure his release on the basis of the Nazi-Soviet Non-Aggression Pact – if only in the spirit of it since there were no provisions that covered such matters. When he learned that his driver was to be released, Anastazy wrote a note to Zofia and asked him to deliver it to her. The rail stop in Brest (today in Belarus), then the border between the two invading armies, was the station where the NKVD turned over captured Polish soldiers to the Germans in December. It was there that the driver, seeing soldiers and "fearing discovery" (as the story went), memorized the note and chewed it up and swallowed it. He recited the message to Zofia when they met. The message to her was that Anastazy had been taken prisoner and that she and their children, fifteen-year-old Maria and fourteen-year-old Henryk, should return to her parents' home in Lemkenmühl (Lamk), and he would return to them there when he was released from captivity after the war. During

World War I, he had been captured by the British and released at the war's end. Release was a reasonable expectation. Just wait out the war. But Anastazy was under arrest as a political prisoner by the Soviet NKVD. Not just a different war now, but a very different captor with an unexpectedly monstrous agenda. Yet, this simple message could have been contained in any postcard or letter Anastazy could have written to Zofia. He was permitted to write a letter or postcard until March, three months after his driver was freed with the note.

What is curious in this account is that he was released when Anastazy was not. The driver was employed by the Polish National Police to assist in moving confidential records out of the country quickly during foreign invasion. It has always been assumed he was a civilian employee, and for that reason, the Soviets may have treated him differently from a police officer, more like a Polish army private or non-comm. They processed him initially as an enemy prisoner of war, and he was imprisoned with Anastazy.

From Zofia's story, we know that at some time, probably after December 1939, the driver delivered a message to her, a note that was supposedly written by Anastazy. The driver carried it from Anastazy to a POW transfer point, voluntarily destroyed it and then recited the message to Zofia when he found her at home in Toruń. Zofia never saw any note, so unknown is whether there ever was a physical note, much less its contents other than as represented by the driver. The message content made sense, given Anastazy's familiarity with World War I.

But the role of the driver is open to question. Zofia never expressed to her daughter any doubt as to the driver's identity or truthfulness. Perhaps she had met the driver prior to their departure or had received correspondence from Anastazy mentioning the driver and urging her to trust him. As noted above (Chapter Seven – "The Families in the New Poland"), the summer of 1939 was a period of increased foreign intelligence activity in Poland as Europe prepared for war. Today's friend might be tomorrow's enemy, so it was important to continue to monitor communications and keep operatives and sources in place to provide a steady stream of intelligence that could be of value when diplomacy fails. In the fall of 1939, as the Soviets were treating German troops and civilians with what could pass for cordiality between allies, Ursula Maria Kuczynski (also known as Sonja Schultz and Ruth Werner among other aliases), a noted Soviet military spy, was residing in Geneva, Switzerland. From there, she was setting up in Danzig an anti-German resistance group of Communist Party members, almost before the ink was dry on the Nazi-Soviet Non-Aggression Pact and its secret protocol dividing eastern Europe between the two countries. In 1936 she had spent three months in Danzig laying the groundwork for intelligence gathering in anticipation of the coming conflict. Even though the pact ruled out active espionage activities, the Gestapo wasted little time in rounding up communist spies and subversives in Germany and abroad.[31] Once the secret protocols of the Non-Aggression Pact became known, the importance of intelligence-gathering took a back seat to the military, and confusion by commanders on all sides was common, especially as Soviet forces invaded Poland. It is possible that the driver was an intelligence agent in the service of the Germans or the Soviets. Or both.[32]

Any suspicion with regard to the driver's true allegiance is further fueled by the fact that the NKVD and Gestapo held a series of conferences starting in September 1939, the purpose of which was to exchange ideas and methods for the occupation of the former Polish state. Both sides expected resistance

---

[31] Ben McIntyre, *Agent Sonya: Moscow's Most Daring Wartime Spy* (New York, Penguin Random House, 2020), p. 173.

[32] A distant cousin of Anastazy's was reportedly an agent doubled against the Soviets.

to occupation, and each could contribute ideas on how best to stifle opposition. The driver's role could have been determined or confirmed by this cooperation between two similar organizations, especially if he had been employed by one of them. In the November meeting, they discussed ways to exchange POWs, which was done in December at Brest when the driver consumed the message.

It will never be known for certain whether he was an innocent caught up in the NKVD net. Zofia was at that point still living in Toruń in Danzig-West Prussia under the civil administration of the Reich. From his likely release in Brest, he had to first cross the General Government area of occupation and either the Reichsgau Wartheland or the province of East Prussia in the Reich to report to her. The timing of his release from Ostashkov is uncertain, but it coincides with verified events. The nameless, faceless driver has become something of a family hero for his service as a courier of news about Anastazy.

This story of the driver, now more than three-quarters of a century after the fact, still remains unverified as to the truth of some of its finer, if fundamental points. The story is symbolic of the confusion of nationality/race and class realities compounded by military and civilian intelligence-gathering activities underway in the occupied areas of eastern Europe, where agreed-upon borders between allies were not always observed but adjusted with the stroke of a pen after the fact of a gun.

Zofia learned from the driver that her husband was a POW in the hands of the NKVD, probably in December 1939. She took the purported advice of Anastazy, and she and their children moved in with her parents in Lemkenmühl, but as the war continued, she started to have doubts as to his safety when rumors started about the execution of Polish prisoners by the Soviets and the disappearance of people to Siberia.

Was she a wife or a widow?

The first news of his death was via her brother-in-law, Klemens. His brother-in-law, Hannelore's brother, reportedly learned from the German government of the discovery at Katyń in 1943. Hannelore had two brothers in the Luftwaffe, both officers, one a major, the other a captain (both spelling their surnames in a German fashion – Pikarski, not Piekarski). This was a case of an ethnic German woman married to a Pole, with information flowing from the Nazi government to a Polish national in the Reichsgau through his wife and her brothers. How easily could these bureaucracies provide information for individuals in a time of war? This was not much different from the case of the driver (presumably an ethnic Pole, or at least not an ethnic German) and his wife (reportedly an ethnic German), who was able to get her husband released by petitioning authorities so soon after civil occupation (established October 8, 1939) was in place in the Reichsgau, and obtaining his freedom from the NKVD. However, only after 1940 was a Nazi bureaucracy firmly in place, making such requests potentially easier. This channel claimed by the family has never been confirmed, and once again – like the driver's wife able to free her husband from the NKVD – it seems odd that the information would flow in that direction through those channels in the chaotic circumstances of the early days of occupation.

Zofia never received official notification of her husband's fate, so after the war she petitioned the local (Toruń, Poland) court for a determination or declaration of death. The court declared on March 3, 1952, that Anastazy died at midnight on May 9, 1946. Of course, by that date, he had been dead already six years, but no one in that Polish government would acknowledge what had really happened to twenty-two thousand Polish officers, police, intellectuals, government officials, politicians and citizens. Forty years after that court declaration, only after the collapse of communism in the Soviet Union and Poland, was the truth revealed and Soviet guilt admitted.[33] But for years after the official declaration bedraggled, cadaverous Polish veterans released from the Soviet gulags would come to Zofia's door and claim to have seen Anastazy alive in the camps.

Was the driver the first of those?

———

Events of 1943 marked the beginning of a period of more hope for family members after the shock of the discovery of the Katyń massacre. In April, about a month after Essen started to feel the most devastating attacks of the war, Johann is reported to have made successful efforts to have Władysław and Klara released from the camps. In the family, it is believed that both Władysław and Klara were in the camps for three years. Again, the story of his friendship with Himmler colors the family narrative of their return, though again without substantiation. Whatever the reason, their release after three years of confinement indicates that the couple was no longer deemed a threat to society beyond camp walls. Their sons were returned to them, and the family moved back to Warlubie, where they had settled when they bought the store they had owned before the war.

Another factor in their release may have been efforts on the part of some Nazis to cultivate support from the Poles after the disclosure of the Katyń massacre. Hans Frank, the Governor-General of the General Government, urged Hitler to lighten policies toward the Poles, but with no apparent success. Frank attempted to curry more favor with the Poles, hoping that would lessen the vigorous underground opposition to his government and even create some semblance of

---

[33] In 2010, a monument to Anastazy was constructed as part of a nationwide program to recognize the victims of Katyń. His monument was placed in the village schoolyard of Skorzewo, where his sister Maria's husband had served as the schoolmaster.

cooperation between Poles and Germany against the advancing Soviets. It was an opening that quickly closed in terms of policy changes but may have figured in the release of some dissidents such as Władysław and Klara.

A recently discovered document, hitherto unknown to the family, casts some doubt on the family belief that imprisonment of both parents lasted three years. In March of 1972, Klara filed a petition for compensation (*Antrag um Entschädigung*) to the German government through the International Tracing Service in Bad Arolsen. In it, she stated that she was a prisoner at Ravensbrück after her arrest by the Gestapo in Warlubie on April 14, 1940, to December 23, 1941. She asserted that her health was lost as a result of hard labor and that she deserved financial reparations. According to the petition, she suffered gastric ailments and required surgery after discharge from the camp. By her own statement, she was released from Ravensbrück 20 months after arrest and confinement, but her return to the family may have been delayed by the surgery and recuperation. Was she released because of illness and disability? Władysław may have been detained for three years, but not Klara, the political, and their sons may have been separated until their father returned from the Neuengamme labor camp.

It was unclear whether Władysław and Klara played any role in the operation of the store on their return, but in 1942 it was still being operated as a store and inn with five bedrooms on the first floor. In addition to metal goods, the proprietor, Albert Laskowski, also sold *Kolonialwaren* (groceries, provisions) out of the store, according to a directory of the time. The happy reunion of the family and their return to Warlubie after three years of separation was clouded by Władysław's and Klara's frail health as well as the loss of ownership of the store. Three years of forced labor in a brickworks under harsh conditions had debilitated him dramatically, and Klara's health as well suffered significantly from her confinement. Nevertheless, Władysław had survived imprisonment at Sachsenhausen and Neuengamme, a feat not accomplished by tens of thousands of Poles, Jews, Roma and Russian POWs whose lives had ended there. Czesław and Zbigniew had studied and learned safely in the German schools, with fluency in German that served them for their entire lives, and they had avoided the camps.

Klemens and Hannelore had served well as Zbigniew's foster parents for the years Władysław and Klara were in the forced labor camps. Klemens seemed to have been sufficiently German for the Nazis to allow him and his wife to foster Zbigniew, but he would demonstrate that under that affected German skin, he was still a Kashub.

Johann and Leocadia, for the five months of the Battle of the Ruhr during 1943, were subjected to almost nightly bombings by the British and daylight bombings by the Americans. Homes all around them were being reduced to rubble by the raids, but their home was untouched, even though half of Essen's buildings were destroyed by the war's end. Fortunately, their daughters and grandchildren were safely far away from them.

———

The next two years would see some changes in the resistance to occupation, as the Polish underground groups, now mostly amalgamated under the Home Army (*Armia Krajowa – AK*), believed the Germans were on the run. Those groups became emboldened, escalating their campaigns from diver-sionary tactics, sabotage and intelligence-gathering activities to outright attacks on German troops in anticipation of the expected imminent collapse of Nazi power, when they would increase their military actions. By August of 1944, the Home Army had four hundred thousand soldiers in its organization after being formed two years earlier and attracting many of the smaller resistance groups. Failed uprisings in the Warsaw Ghetto in April 1943 and the unsuccessful attempt by the Home Army to liberate Warsaw in August 1944 proved that the collapse of the Nazis was not as imminent as thought and that the Soviets, despite great successes in pushing westward, were not interested in supporting the Home Army in liberating Warsaw.

Over the next two years, some members of the Kiedrowski family were encouraged as well by what they regarded as the palpable decline in Nazi strength in both the General Government and annexed territories. But like the experience of the Home Army, even late in 1944 there was miscalculation on how hard they could poke the bear of Nazi order.

On March 2, 1944,[34] Anastazy's widow Zofia was arrested by the Danzig Gestapo at her home in Lemkenmühl, where she was living with her two teenagers, Maria and Henryk. According to records, she supported "communist gangs" and was sent to Stutthof concentration camp, where she was assigned prisoner number 33785 on entry on April 6, 1944, identified as a political prisoner. Based on what we know now and what she suspected then – that her husband had been executed by the Soviets – it seems unlikely that she would have joined communist groups. In fact, she was a supporter (if not member) of *TOW Gryf Pomorski* (*Tajna Organizacja Wojskowa Gryf Pomorski* – Secret Military Organization of the Pomeranian Griffin).

The Pomeranian Griffin organization was a pro-church, strongly nationalist group. Created July 7, 1941, *Gryf Pomorski* was a successor organization to *Gryf Kaszubski* (Kashubian Griffin), which had expanded its activities well beyond the

---

[34] Five days later, on March 7, her father-in-law, Anton Lew von Kiedrowski, the patriarch of the family, died in Schöndorf (Kurkowo) at the age of ninety-one.

area of Kashubia. GP's membership has been estimated to have been at least eight thousand, perhaps as high as nineteen thousand. Of that number, approximately five hundred were active in the forests of Pomerania, in dozens of bunkers and shelters. It was a resistance organization whose activities were largely confined to areas annexed to the Reich and was a smaller version of the AK which functioned almost exclusively in the General Government. Resistance operations were much riskier in the annexed lands of the Reich than in the General Government.

Zofia was arrested by the Gestapo in a dragnet set out for hundreds of suspected Pomeranian Griffin members in three counties, one of which was Chojnice, where she lived. As many as three thousand were arrested in the spring of 1944 after the Gestapo got hold of a membership list. Initially, they were jailed in Danzig for a short time, then sent to Stutthof, as Zofia was. Records at Stutthof don't reveal how long Zofia was confined there, but it is recalled by the family that she was only confined a short time – a month or two. However, her arrest as a resistance member, even for so short a time, would create problems for her and her family in postwar communist Poland. The values she shared with Pomeranian Griffin – pro-Catholic and pro-Poland and Kashubian, and as a result of her husband's fate, most likely anti-communist – would not be favorably viewed by the postwar communist government. Many former partisans, whether from the annexed lands or the General Government, were viewed by Polish security forces as threats to the new regime, and membership lists discovered by the Gestapo probably did not vanish with the end of the war and regime change. They served as protection from prosecution for past transgressions or even tickets to new careers in the communist security apparatus.

During this period of increased activity by Pomeranian Griffin and the simultaneous Gestapo dragnets, Klemens and a priest friend – whose name has been lost to history – were celebrating a birthday and enjoying adult beverages in a church in Bromberg (Bydgoszcz). Passersby complained that the two inebriated pals were singing boisterously, extolling the greatness of Poland in addition to proclaiming musically "Kashubia forever and forever a Kashub" (*Wiedno Kaszëbë i na wiedno Kaszëbi*). The public complaints were directed to the local police. The priest managed to retreat to the church as a sanctuary, but Klemens was arrested by the authorities for asocial behavior colored by political misconduct, and consigned to Stutthof.

Most Nazi concentration camps had sub-camps or satellites affiliated with them. Stutthof, in addition to the old camp opened in 1939, had as many as forty affiliated sites, some associated with industrial enterprises, and not all were close to the main camp. In Bromberg, there were two Stutthof sub-camps, including Bromberg-Ost, which had been set up in the summer of 1944 exclusively for women for the repair and maintenance of the rail system, and another that had been established at a large munitions factory (*DAG Fabrik Bromberg*) and for at least two years had been using thousands of concentration camp prisoners and POWs, as well as locals.

No one today recalls whose birthday was being celebrated (Klemens' birth date was January 16, 1897), or when the celebration actually took place, but since it was in Bromberg (Bydgoszcz) rather than in Klemens' hometown of Dirschau (Tczew), it was most likely the observance of the priest's birth or his name day.[35] Name days were traditionally celebrated more vigorously than birthday anniversaries. The story of Klemens' arrest and confinement has more color than detail, but it is believed that he spent a year in a Stutthof labor camp

---

[35] Klemens's name day was November 23, and interestingly, St. Clements was the patron saint of metal workers and blacksmiths. Klemens, of course, before the war had been a partner in the Lietz and Kiedrowski ironworks.

and then escaped, most likely while being transported, whether on foot or by train. By late 1944 the Red Army was approaching rapidly, and the main camp and others in the path of the Soviets were being evacuated by marches to the west to Germany or north to the Baltic for evacuation by boat, or simply for execution by machine-guns after being forced into the water. The evacuation of Stutthof and some of its sub-camps began in late January 1945, when the main camp still held fifty thousand prisoners. As the Allies closed in on Germany, labor and death camps were emptied so that the Allies would not capture the camps with inmates or any evidence of atrocities. Nor did the Soviets want survivors from the camps, lest they become heroes and interfere with Stalin's plans for the new Polish state. There were death marches from a number of those camps, as many of the starved inmates in frail health died on the road or were executed when they couldn't keep pace with the column.

By the end of 1944, a large number of POW laborers were included in the five thousand total workers at DAG Bromberg. However he managed to escape from custody, Klemens turned up on the doorstep of Władysław and Klara in Warlubie likely in January 1945, some 75 km from Bromberg.[36] He was louse-ridden and hungry. Klara apparently resisted the urge to burn his clothes (which "moved on their own", as she later remarked) but washed them thoroughly, and he hid with the family until the war was over.

There is no surviving record of Klemens being committed to the camp, nor is there any record of him in any available collections of camp inmates. He was arrested by local police who, in view of the political nature of his singing, turned him

---

[36] Had he escaped from the main camp at Stutthof, his trip would have been nearly twice as long – about 140 km – and would have taken him through his hometown of Dirschau, where he might have found sanctuary with family or friends.

over to the Gestapo. It is believed by the family that Klemens spent about a year in Stutthof before escaping and living out the war in hiding at his brother's home. Since evacuations from Stutthof Main Camp began in earnest in late January 1945 as the Red Army rolled through occupied Poland, that gives a possible timeline for Klemens to have the opportunity to flee from custody, and then applying the "year" of captivity takes us back to January 1944, as the likely earliest time of arrest. The city of Bromberg was liberated by the Red Army on January 23, 1945. The excitement of liberation and the confusion it caused created ideal opportunities for captives to escape. Officially, the Red Army liberated all occupied Poland by March 1945, with the exception of the Stutthof Main Camp, which was not liberated by the Soviets until May 9, 1945, by which time it was virtually empty.

What this story lacks in detail is made up for in what it provides in terms of the family's recall of Klemens' personality and illustrates what many Poles experienced during those times.

———

The defeat at Stalingrad, while affecting the course of the war, also gave new hope to the resistance organizations throughout occupied and annexed Poland. No longer were the Nazi occupiers invincible. Kiedrowski family members acted on their own hopes as well, having been staggered by the news of Katyń.

In the spring of 1940, Stalin at last achieved vengeance for the Polish-Soviet War of 1921 by sabotaging the creation of any future Polish state by pre-emptively decapitating it, creating a vacuum he could fill in the future with his hand-picked protégés. But it took the victory at Stalingrad to validate his desired status as hegemon of eastern Europe and champion of the working class. The cautious optimism that seemed to grow after the Nazi defeat at Stalingrad in February 1943 and the Allied invasion of Normandy in June 1944 seemed to reach its apogee as the Red Army liberated Poland. By the summer of 1944, there was widespread optimism, celebration and even euphoria in Poland. Little thought was given to what would happen when the Soviets replaced the Nazis as occupiers of Poland.

In the wake of liberation came ethnic cleansing with the approval and even encouragement of the victorious powers in conference at Yalta in February, and later at Potsdam in July and August. One oppressive regime was exchanged for another. Few expected the misery and brutality that would follow the war's end. None of the brothers nor their sister or their families would escape the peace that followed, the peace that millions had sought after years of war, but a peace that betrayed those hopes.

CHAPTER TEN
Surviving the Peace

By May 8, 1946, the first anniversary of VE-Day, Sigmund still had no direct news of his family in Germany or Poland. But the newspapers, radio broadcasts and theater news films were filled with reports of massive destruction, staggering privation and the expulsion of ethnic Germans from eastern Europe.

The war had dramatically changed the map of Europe. Germany and Poland, in particular, were now defined by new borders, both losing land area. Populations were moved into newly-configured states to make them ethnically homogeneous. All of Woodrow Wilson's "troublesome friends, the Poles", would now be enclosed to the exclusion of other ethnicities in a state firmly affixed to the Soviet Union. The city of Danzig, now renamed Gdańsk, exemplified the victorious allies' policy of ethnic cleansing. Germans had played a significant role in the city's life for hundreds of years. By the time the Soviets entered the burned-out city in March of 1945, the few remaining ethnic German inhabitants were eager to escape; those that hadn't were deported to Germany by the provisional Polish government. The massive St Mary's Lutheran Church, one of the largest Gothic brick churches in the world when it was completed in 1502, was re-consecrated as a Catholic cathedral after the Polish government gave it to the diocese in 1955.

The twelve million Germans expelled from their ancestral homes were almost without exception moved to the British, French or American zones of West Germany. Pomerania constituted a large portion of the "recovered" western territories, and it was not unusual there for Kashubs, Poles and Germans to find themselves in villages still occupied by the Red Army and the ever-present NKVD. Ethnic Germans being forcibly displaced from what had become western

Poland were not always removed as quickly as authorities desired, and Poles and Kashubs occasionally came into contact with the former owners of the land they had been given. The Kashubs were native to the area, but many of the incoming Poles had been evicted from their villages in eastern Poland, now Belorussia and Ukraine. Kashubs often found themselves mediating between those from the East, and the ethnic Germans who managed to stay behind because they were somewhat Polonized or had skills valued by the government. Being insufficiently German for the Germans and insufficiently Polish for the Poles put the Kashubs in a unique position to reconcile parties in the ethnic turmoil that followed the end of the war. Each side could view the Kashubs with less animosity than might have been the case with other likely mediators, German, Polish or Russian.

The United States, in contrast to Europe and its six-year nightmare, emerged from its three-and-a-half year participation with casualties less than one percent of its population. But for many German-American immigrants – the largest number of citizens of European ethnicity in America – the war's end was only a beginning to what stagger those who had downplayed their ancestry during the war. Civilian correspondence between Germany and America had been virtually non-existent from 1939 through the war, and lack of communication persisted well beyond the conclusion of hostilities. Consequently, most German-Americans had little if any idea of what was happening to their relatives abroad. Many had family behind in the rubble that was now Germany, in which nearly all of Europe's ethnic Germans were to be concentrated in a land area twenty-five percent less than before the war.

Sigmund shared those concerns of many of the tens of millions of Americans of German heritage as they waited to learn of the fate of their relatives. Not only was Germany's industrial capacity shattered and military destroyed, but population centers were leveled, and even more needy civilians were now being transferred into the cities that lay in ruins. For Sigmund, having close family in a severely de-populated Poland with new borders was only one concern. The expulsion of ethnic Germans from within that new state, transferring Poles to the western areas, and the political churning of eastern Europe as the Soviets tightened control of governments, could only intensify his dread and uncertainty.

His business had prospered immediately after the war as soldiers returned, became engaged, and married – which led to the purchase of luxury items in numbers long depressed before and during the war. Marriages and household formations now suddenly spiked. Those new households produced children in booming numbers. Money for non-essential products, so absent during the Depression and the war, was becoming more available as the postwar American economy expanded as well. But no matter how flush Sigmund felt personally, he was anxious to hear from relatives.

From late 1942 into 1944, gasoline was strictly rationed, virtually banning pleasure driving in the U.S. During the last year of the war and immediately after, Sigmund had experienced a troubling recurring sight on the rare Sunday family drive in the old gray Plymouth. In Minnesota, there were some fifteen prisoners of war camps, and most of them provided labor (paid in scrip) to farmers and loggers who were feeling the shortage of able-bodied workers caused by the war. Sigmund's daughter, Gretchen, observed him as he gazed on the field workers with "PW" on their shirt backs, saying with his eyes what he never spoke: "There but for the grace of God go I." Was there anyone among the PW's in that field from Essen? Might they know his brother or his family? What had they heard from their families? His decision to leave family and the familiar behind on a journey in 1923 to an unknown country was without a doubt now – if not before – although the most difficult, by far the best of his life. Men his age and older were conscripted into Hitler's military as the Third Reich collapsed into smoldering ruins, a fate he had escaped.

But his family was still there.

The first family news came from a familiar source. Sigmund's nephew, Hans von Loewe, son of Sigmund's brother Johann, learned in the summer of 1946 of the family casualties. In May he had written to his parents in Essen. His mother, Leocadia, responding to that letter shortly after receiving it in July, told him of his father's death from heart failure. He weighed just 105 lbs. when he died. This was a man who, though not tall, weighed 220 lbs. before the war, even when he was struggling with heart health issues. The sad news cascaded off the page from the cramped writing and scribbles in the margins, all in German that Leocadia struggled to write. In that letter, Hans also learned of the death of his younger brother, Heinz, who had died as an infantryman in January 1945. He had died in the field hospital in Bad Münstereifel and was buried in the military cemetery there with four hundred seventy-six other German casualties, most of whom died in the Battle of the Hürtgen Forest a battle of little consequence with thousands of casualties. Originally in a mass grave, he was moved to an individual one in 1953.[37]

Johann had declined rapidly after learning of Heinz's death and burial in a mass grave. Leocadia wrote bitterly that on the wartime rations of Germany at that time (even for someone with presumed local political connections through his job at Essen transit), Johann was on a near-starvation diet and died in the hospital after suffering a stroke. This first news came to Sigmund from Hans, who knew how close Sigmund and Johann had been.

An even more depressing letter to Hans was written by

---

[37] According to *Deutsche Dienststelle*, private letter to author, June 24, 2009.

Irmgard, Hans' elder sister, who listed nine friends who did not return from the war, some dead, some missing already for years, or likely in Siberia. Her own husband, Hugo F, returned in September of 1945 from being a Russian prisoner of war, weakened but alive. She and her children had spent nearly three years in southern Germany in "two nice rooms", as she put it, with a chief forester in Bavaria, away from the worst of the bombing, and none of the family were casualties of the bombing. Over the next eighteen months, letters from his family to Hans painted a grim picture of occupied Germany.

Hunger dominated the content of letters received by Hans, whether from his mother, sisters or brothers-in-law. There had been essentially no harvest in Germany in 1945 since Allied forces were pushing from east and west in the spring planting season, and farmers fled their farms in advance of the invasion. Leocadia, in her first letter in response to Hans' promise of food, suggested that nothing worth more than the local equivalent of fifteen dollars be sent otherwise customs duty would be high. In addition to food, such everyday items as shaving soap, razor blades, toothpaste, shoelaces, stockings and darning cotton were in short supply, and his family sought them as well as shirt collars and studs for the men who were fortunate enough to hold office jobs that required proper apparel. The rationing of food was severe, but no food could be sent from America to Germany until December 1945, complicated by the need to move ships from the Pacific after the Japanese surrender in order to carry food to Europe. Moreover, the output from the German economy was abysmally low and lacked a reliable distribution network since the robust German rail system and rollingstock had been devastated by Allied bombing. On the weekends, the remaining trains of ramshackle passenger cars, themselves picked clean of anything of value, were packed with city-dwellers traveling to the countryside over the crumbling remnants of local roadbed to obtain produce in exchange for the few earthly possessions they still had. Work absenteeism increased as bartering with farmers became a more reliable source of food than wages, and urban workers did not wait for the weekend for their trips to the countryside to scrounge whatever provisions they could. The greatest food shortages were in the urban areas. The rural areas, in some cases, had as much or more food than before the war once farming was resumed. The feeling widespread among the Germans (as expressed in letters to Hans) was that the farmers were doing well – all the wealth was leaving the cities and going to the rural areas where, as Leocadia wrote, the city dwellers suspected that "cow-stalls had carpet and pigs wore earrings".

Adults were allotted one thousand calories per day in the first year of occupation. In his letter of October 11, 1946, Hildegard's husband, Hans, listed the rationing for those without special needs or privileges:

> Bread 3 pounds every week
> 62.5 gr butter or margarine every two weeks,
> plus once a month, 70 gr
> 1 lb. grain per month (corn meal or barley)
> 600 grams of fish per month
> 450 grams of meat per month
> 3 / 4 pounds of sugar per month
> 62.5 grams of cheese per month
> 1 pound of jam per month
> 16 pounds of potatoes per month [38]

He observed that many Germans envied the pigs who were allotted 2000 lbs. of potatoes per year, while the humans got less than 200 lbs. Deliveries of the food rations were frequently weeks behind, and fat was in especially short

---

[38] For reasons best known to himself, he mixed metric and English measurements, using the abbreviation for Pfund (pound) and no mention of kilograms.

supply as well, rationed at 50 grams (less than 2 oz.) per week, an amount which before the war it was not unusual to consume in a single meal.

After years of war, there were shortages not only of food, but clothing as well. Shoes and coats were becoming an item of concern as winter approached in 1946. Hans' sister, Irmgard, wrote that her son, Manfred, hadn't gotten a pair of shoes in two-and-a-half years, and he was eight. His little sister Christa (age two and a half) had no coat. Hans was encouraged to send used items – stockings, shoes, coats – so there would be no duty levied on them.

Food packages were predominantly CARE packages, which only after June of 1946 could be sent to occupied Germany.[39] Leocadia received the first package from Sigmund on December 16, Hildegard received her first on the 21st and Irmgard two days later. Between that December and April, 1947 Sigmund would send at least ten packages to family, all in the British Zone. It took as long as two months for some of the packages to arrive after ordering and paying in advance. In addition to providing badly-needed food for survivors, the CARE packages were guaranteed to reach the intended recipients as long as a former address was provided and thus were a useful method of tracing displaced persons. The donors received a typewritten receipt signed by the intended recipient as proof of delivery.

By October 1946, Leocadia had received a package of food from Sigmund, as well as from her son's in-laws. Leocadia was one of the lucky citizens of Essen whose address had not changed, so any packages sent did not have to be forwarded, which could delay delivery. That convivial apartment at Katzenbruchstrasse, where Sigmund had spent many visits on his way in or out of Europe, had been destroyed by a direct hit

---

[39] CARE was the Cooperative for American Remittances to Europe Inc., a humanitarian group formed to prevent the spread of starvation in Europe.

during the war. Fortunately, the new home at Lehnsgrund 52 in Margarethenhöhe that Leocadia and Johann had moved to in October 1938 had been spared destruction.

Sigmund learned that sending green, unroasted coffee beans was the better way to provide real caffeine, since there apparently was little or no duty on them for the recipients, and they were less likely to be "lost" by postal workers, whether sent to Germany or Poland. This "bean coffee" was extraordinarily prized by Leocadia, especially over what she called "German Coffee" made from grain and chicory. This first package sent to her was in all likelihood some sort of ad hoc combination that Sigmund had cobbled together, including coffee, sugar, and chocolate, since CARE packages he sent had not yet reached her. The packages were "10-in-1" packages that were military surplus, left over from preparations for the invasion of Japan. They could support ten persons for one day or one person for ten days, containing meat and meat products, margarine, sugar, chocolate, powdered eggs, coffee and several other items, nearly 20 lbs. of food. They cost the sender $10.00. Of the receipts that survived to this day, two packages were also sent to the von Pikarski family, most likely in-laws of Klemens, and another two to an Elisabeth Wendt, a woman unidentified by family.

Any package from America was awaited with great anticipation and received joyously by the intended recipients

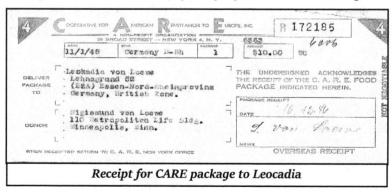

Receipt for CARE package to Leocadia

who would receive advance word in the donor's name that a package was on its way. Occasionally one might go astray, but it was rare. Leocadia gushed gratitude to her son, urging him not to spend so much, since he had a wife and newborn son to take care of. On one occasion, however, she suggested that Sigmund wasn't doing enough, thinking himself "better" than them. Sigmund, in fact, was sending CARE packages to people other than her family. By April of 1947, Hans had sent twenty-two packages, so by that standard, Sigmund's six to the family during that period made him seem like a cheapskate. Not all packages received by the family in Essen were CARE, however. Special needs like men's dress shirts, detachable collars, stockings, etc., often made up a package sent privately through normal postal channels.

The winter of 1946-7 was a horrendous one in occupied Germany – *der Hungerwinter*. A hot, dry summer with drought, which substantially reduced crop yields, was followed by a late but bitterly cold winter. Food shortages led to riots in some cities in the spring of 1947. Typhus and tuberculosis were widespread among a population weakened by hunger and cold. Late in 1947, even potatoes – a staple of the German diet – were becoming scarce due to a crop failure. The seed potatoes were now being consumed for food, putting future crops in jeopardy. Hans's response to this crisis was quite extraordinary. He ordered 400 lbs. of potatoes in the Netherlands for delivery to his family in Essen. That was more than double the annual ration for an adult. His family was understandably thrilled at the news.

Of all the shortages, one of the most curious was that of envelopes. In May of 1947, there were no letter envelopes to be had in Essen. Although businesses and individuals mailing within Germany could get by without envelopes for their letters by simply folding the letter, gluing it together, and writing the address on the blank back of the stationery, that method was unreliable for international mail. Sometimes the family in Essen would write a couple of letters and then scrounge an envelope and mail them together. Other times, letters simply weren't written until they got their hands on an envelope. In at least one letter, Hans' brother-in-law Hugo asked that envelopes be sent in the next package. Leocadia groused that only the miners could get them. In general, those employed in heavy labor, especially the mining, iron and steel industries, which were targeted by the German government and occupation authorities for special treatment to re-build the economy, had more access to coffee, sugar, brandy and bacon than others in Germany, and apparently office supplies as well.

The German economy had become a barter economy, with local currency of little value in obtaining essentials of life. Price controls instituted by Hitler in 1936 and rationing initiated in 1939 were continued under the occupation. A weak currency exacerbated the situation. Hans S observed in a letter to his brother-in-law that Hans von Loewe's attitude toward smoking had changed from the last time he was in Germany (1934) when he insisted that S pay for his own cigarettes even though Hans was paying for everything else. The war had changed many things. Notwithstanding price controls and rationing intended to improve the currency's stability, coffee and cigarettes became the coin of the occupied realm. Unfortunately, cigarettes came through with a high tariff after the first twenty pieces (a single pack), 47 pfennigs apiece. But it was valuable currency in great demand. Johann's grave could not be finished until his widow came up with eighty cigarettes. Leocadia had all her teeth pulled, and the dentist demanded cigarettes to make the dentures. A pair of real shoes for Irmgard's son, Manfred, would have cost 400 marks – but only one pound of coffee. However, in late November of 1947, Leocadia wrote that she heard on the radio that cigarettes and coffee sent by mail would be confiscated.

When it became known that the Marshall Plan was in the

works, there was a great deal of excitement. It had been delayed because of opposition to aiding the country that had been responsible for starting the war. The Plan would not be passed by the U.S. Congress until April 1948, but a three hundred-million-dollar loan to the Ruhr region for re-building the industrial capacity destroyed by the war was made before that, according to Irmgard's husband, Hugo. After the second consecutive summer of crop failure in 1947, in his letter of November 26, 1947, Hugo wrote that the family cried that the Marshall Plan was their "sole hope in the current sad existence". It was the Christmas wish of all.

———

But Sigmund's family in Poland had little to look forward to.

When the Marshall Plan took hold in Europe by late 1948 (but not in Poland), Sigmund's attention and activities could be more focused on Poland and his family there, but until then, he was torn between the two extended family groups and between what was needed and what was possible, the former common in the two countries, the latter not.

A report received from a surprising correspondent confirmed his worst fears. In October of 1946, a more complete list of family casualties, this time from the Polish side, was delivered in an unexpected letter to Sigmund. It first staggered and then stirred him to action he might never have anticipated, action that could affect not just himself but potentially the well-being of his wife and children. As he opened the letter from his niece, Maria, Anastazy's daughter, living in Poland, the news was shattering. Sigmund's family in Germany and Poland knew his address only as his business address: 110 Metropolitan Building, Minneapolis, Minnesota. That had been unchanged for nearly twenty years as he and Marvyl and family moved from home to home. He read the letter, closed the store (unusual for him) and took the streetcar home to share it with Marvyl, calling ahead to let her know of the letter.

Gretchen recalled that Marvyl quickly shooed her and Karl outside. She did not want them to see their father cry. In that letter, he likely learned of the presumed death of Maria's father Anastazy and of Sigmund's father in 1944 and mother a year later. Of his parents and five surviving siblings whom he had last seen in 1927, there were now only his sister, Maria, and two brothers, Władysław and Klemens, and their respective families.

In his profound grief, Sigmund may not have sensed the mantle of family protector, advocate and supporter that had silently slipped upon his shoulders, initially with imperceptible weight. Ultimately, it would test his resolve with a weight unexpected. He picked up his trusty Sheaffer fountain pen filled with the family's signature green ink and wrote in German:

Nov. 5, 1946

Dear Niece Marie [sic]. I received your letter of 22 October yesterday. I was happy to hear from you but very saddened to hear the reports. If I'm not mistaken, you must be about twenty-two years old now. When I last saw you, you were about three years old. In your letter, you said that you are in need as well as embarrassed [to ask for help]. Never forget that when you are in need, you should first ask your family. Rest assured that whatever can be done will be done. May I ask you, where have you learned to write German? What sort of work do you do now? What is the name of your brother in England, and what does he do there? Now, about help for you and your mother. Neither packages nor money can be sent right now to Poland. As soon as permitted, I will send you fifty dollars, but right now, nothing can be sent from here. But should someone from over there know how I could send money, please let me know. As you wrote me, your brother is in England and has learned nothing. I think I can give some advice – learn a trade! A trade is a golden floor. I myself am a watchmaker. I had to work hard to achieve that. I am also convinced that your father worked hard and was proud of it. Now, when you have time again, write me a few lines, and I will help you however I can.

Now that's enough for today.

Best greetings to you as well as your mother,
Your Uncle Sigismund

PS: Every enclosed [international postal] coupon is just enough for a postage stamp in your post office.

More than a year after the end of World War II, there was no way yet established to send help to family in Poland, a country with no less devastation than apparent in Germany. Its population was in the deepest distress and now essentially occupied by a former enemy invader, an ally of the U.S. Warsaw and the old city of Gdańsk especially had been leveled to an extreme comparable to some of the industrial centers of Germany. Although not as physically devastated as the larger cities, towns and villages were depopulated by the Nazi slave labor policies and the Final Solution. A third of the pre-war population of Poland was gone.

Sigmund was clever and resourceful, someone not averse to circumventing governmental and political restrictions. Unable to send CARE packages to family in Poland, he looked for alternatives and sought a way to send cash, as he mentioned to Maria. His business involved cash, and he felt most comfortable when he had a "Benjamin" or two in his wallet, but sending cash through international mail was risky. There were that many more opportunities for less-than-honorable postal workers along the way to sidetrack the envelope and steal the cash. However, there was no easy way to get money to relatives – personal checks didn't work for individuals using the banking systems of Europe still recovering from the war. By 1948 Sigmund was using a sandwich of ten-dollar bills glued between photos. One such "sandwich" included a photo of the home he and Marvyl had just purchased in 1947, a four-bedroom stucco Tudor style, with his new 1947 Pontiac in the driveway to the two-car garage, and a photo of him relaxing in an overstuffed chair in the living room.

The cash – American dollars – had greater value than the official exchange rate for local currency, since it was hard currency, i.e., still backed by gold at that time and widely usable outside its country of origin, especially in black market transactions. Sending a package containing green coffee beans with a few bills mixed in with the beans was another ploy that could work – combining two highly-prized commodities.

One of Sigmund's most-inspired but least-useful packages sent to Poland was one of silk neckties, which he urged Władysław and Klemens to sell or use as barter for needed items. Both had experience as tradespeople and businessmen, and it may have seemed logical to give them the opportunity to make some money from a luxury product. They sought to explain to Sigmund that in the "workers' paradise" of Poland, silk neckties were considered bourgeois and therefore inappropriate and of little value. It was definitely different from S's and F's need for detachable collars and studs in West Germany. Neckties did offer a fine vehicle to conceal cash, but Sigmund's well-intentioned action didn't work.

For Klemens and his wife Hannelore, the situation was no less dire, even with no children. After the war and the imposition of the communist government, Klemens was employed in the state-owned ironworks that he and Adolph Lietz had founded and owned since the 1920s. From owner to employee was a huge change, but one that was not unknown in the People's Poland of the late 1940s. Private enterprise officially no longer existed. The state owned everything, and there were few opportunities for advancement for former entrepreneurs except as a member of the state apparatus governing the economy. That was not for Klemens. He chafed under state control, and eventually, he and Hannelore left Poland for Germany.

Władysław and Klara had fewer options. Both were suffering from poor health after years in the camps, and their now teenage sons Czesław and Zbigniew made leaving Poland impractical. Their futures seemed to be in Poland, communist or not. Their mobility was virtually non-existent. While Klemens and Hannelore could claim some German connection through her family who had left Poland for the British Zone of Germany, Władysław and his family would have found it difficult to leave Poland for Germany. Although all four could speak German thanks to camp imprisonment and Nazi occupation, taking a family of four out of its home country and applying for citizenship in another country totally alien to them (and one for which they had well-earned hostility) was not a viable option. There was no known family connection other than Leocadia, widow of Władysław's brother, and she wasn't well-equipped to adopt a family; she had her own children and grandchildren who needed attention, and her own health was not good. They would be on their own with the head of the family in frail health. Were there jobs for them there? Germany was being inundated by the ethnic Germans from eastern Europe, millions of immigrants, displaced persons and refugees in desperate need of food and housing. In fact, other than escaping the Stalinist terror endemic in the new People's Poland following the referendum of June 1946 and the January 1947 elections, immediate benefits would be small, as they would be swallowed up in the horde of other immigrants to West Germany also seeking new lives.

Sigmund had been sending packages and concealed money, but he began to feel that he needed to do something more. The necktie idea didn't fly, failing even on the black market. There were few options, since CARE packages could not be sent to Poland, and the Marshall Plan, though in the near future, would not extend to Poland. Armed opposition to communist rule continued in Poland, not ending until 1952. Private enterprise was dead. The outlook was bleak for anyone in Poland. And Władysław and his family were in Poland, apparently to stay.

Although the specifics are unclear, what Sigmund undertook in the face of this reality of Władysław and his family was quite extraordinary (and unknown to his children until more than fifty years after his death). Sigmund offered to bring his nephew Czesław to America to live with his family in Minneapolis in their home at 107 Pratt Street, a house that Marvyl had urged Sigmund to buy, a much more elegant home in a much better location than their old home at 4952 Third Ave South, where they had lived for less than five years. The offer was made between late 1946 and late 1948, at which time Czesław would have been eighteen years old. Whether the offer was extended to Zbigniew as well is one of the many details missing. He was two years younger than Czesław. By late 1948, Gretchen was fourteen, Karl seven. The commotion that acceptance would have caused in the von Loewe household was probably nothing compared to what happened in the rural community of Warlubie, Poland, when it was proposed.

Sigmund rarely ignored input from his wife on major decisions. Since his children are unable to this day to recall any discussions, heated or otherwise, of the proposal, suggests that either Marvyl easily acquiesced or was not consulted. The latter seems unlikely. Though no Rosie the Riveter, she was not the stereotypical housewife of the 1940s. She had a career as a singer and a teacher, and had strong opinions on a variety of subjects – often well-thought-out.[40] She may have looked upon this as the *quid* for the *quo* of buying her dream house along the Minnehaha Creek. She had also watched him struggling in the evenings writing letters to family in German (or Polish – a special struggle), often after he had spent post-dinner hours working at that table-top machine shop of a watchmaker's bench in what was the guest bedroom of the home. Moreover, none of her relatives had died in the war or spent time in labor camps, and she, too, had seen the

---

[40] In addition to singing in the quartet at Temple Israel in Minneapolis, where her lyric soprano voice had been heard for nearly fifteen years, she still gave voice lessons two days a week at her studio at MacPhail School of Music.

expression on his face when they drove by German POWs working in the Minnesota fields. It may not have been a struggle for her to agree with his proposal, and she might very well have started working on the logistics of having another teenager in the house and another mouth to feed.

It was about this time that Marvyl told her children that food would take priority in the house over everything else. Sigmund had stated that under no circumstances would there be scrimping on food after what he was learning about his family in Europe. Food came first. While other families recalled the Depression and how it had affected them a decade earlier, and wartime rationing more recently, Sigmund knew of the hunger that his family was experiencing in the painful present. It was closer than he ever wanted it to be, and he would never allow his wife or children to experience real hunger, a hunger that was making his nieces cry as their children begged their mothers for something to eat. "Starving children in Europe" was not an abstract notion for him; it was family.

If the decision-making process leading to the offer was smooth or at least without open expressions of opposition, that was not the case on the other end. Władysław and Klara had strong differences of opinion on how to respond to Sigmund's proposition. Władysław was in favor of the arrangement for reasons unknown for certain, but suspected. What is known is that his health, poor when he returned from Sachsenhausen labor camp, was not improving. The burden of raising two teenage boys in a country that was still recovering from war and occupation may have seemed to be too much for him to ignore in the face of such a generous offer. To assure that one of his sons might be able to escape the difficult times by going to America was an appealing option for the father. He saw it as a chance for success that Czesław might not otherwise have had if he had stayed in Poland.

Klara, on the other hand, was adamantly opposed to

letting even one of her sons leave them for America. She and her husband had been separated from their sons for years while in the labor camps, and the sons had lived with separate families at that time. Even with her health issues, Klara did not want a reprise of that separation. In addition, although Czesław was relatively fluent in German, having been force-fed it for the period of the occupation, and also in Polish, now what was being proposed would necessitate that he learn a third language to live with his Uncle Sigmund and family in America, especially if he wanted to continue his education at the high school level. The cultural differences were huge as well. Living in rural Warlubie in a Poland still struggling to recover from the war and under a communist government, was far different from living in urban Minneapolis in an America that was fast becoming an expanding consumer economy. There was just too much to argue against the offer.

Czesław was never consulted, and in the end Klara persuaded Władysław to decline the proposal, and Czesław remained in Poland, never emigrating. He would continue his higher education, eventually becoming an electrical engineer, marrying an émigré from the Soviet Union, Tamara Zmako, in 1962, and raising their two children in an apartment on Stolarski Street in Gdańsk.

In 2008, the last living source for this story, Czesław himself told it simply with authenticity and without apparent embellishment. There was never a hint of disappointment in missing an opportunity to live in America. Perhaps there was a bit of wistful amusement in thinking of what might have been when he – then in his late 70s – met the possible little brother and sister sixty years after Sigmund's proposal.

Klemens and Hannelore, as well as Władysław and his family, remained in Poland as the Iron Curtain of the Cold War came down on Europe, shutting off not just Poland from any meaningful contact with the west. But Klemens the entrepreneur grew frustrated with the regime in Poland, and he and Hannelore left Poland for Germany about 1950. Sigmund was the sole surviving brother financially capable of assisting his brothers, sister, nieces and nephews, whether in Germany or Poland, and in the latter case, cash seemed to be the best way to help. He was the quintessential American immigrant who sends support home to family left behind in "the old country", whether that country is Poland or Peru.

When he returned to his childhood home in 1927, Sigmund doubtless made an impression on his parents and siblings as he brought them gold pocket watches. The gesture was grand for the youngest of the family who had left them for America. Twenty years later, what he did was no simple gesture. It was instead his expression of a willingness to put at risk a hard-earned, comfortable family life and financial well-being for the benefit of family members who, though staying behind, had experienced the worst aspects of a migrant's life, and repeatedly so. The life disruptions they suffered were in some cases orders of magnitude greater than most migrants, as the very essence of their humanity was repeatedly torn from them and their human dignity stolen time after time.

Sigmund never fully shared with his children his distress over his family in Germany and Poland when their lives were crushed by war, oppression and hunger. When he died in 1958 after a long struggle with asthma and a heart weakened by rheumatic fever as a youth, Marvyl, Gretchen and Karl lost all contact with family in Europe. Sigmund alone had been the correspondent, and Marvyl was crushed by his death, unable to express her grief adequately even to her children, and struggling with closing the store in the doomed Metropolitan Building. Gretchen, newly married, and Karl, a college freshman, were focused on their own lives and had no idea of the extent of their family – especially the Polish one – in Europe. Hans wrote his sisters in Germany immediately, but the family in Poland knew nothing until years later. The roots Sigmund had carefully abandoned in 1923 to facilitate his immigration to America would remain unknown to his children for nearly eighty years, as would his extraordinary efforts to help family members survive a brutal peace.

CHAPTER ELEVEN
The Next Generation

December 15, 1981. As the train shuddered to a stop, the lone passenger hoisted his rucksack, stepped off the carriage onto the platform and walked down the concrete steps to the tunnel under the tracks and past closed shops in the darkened Gdańsk main train station. A three-hour trip had taken nearly ten with several stops and two train changes. Each transfer to another train increased the risk of discovery because, although his exception to the travel ban was clear if anyone used the telephone to check its validity, he could be at the very least detained by the authorities, at worst arrested and jailed once stolen state property was discovered in the rucksack. He had seemed to be the only passenger on this last leg of the trip, and each stop tested his resolve since papers had to be checked repeatedly, and there was no crowd to melt into. There was still a fifteen-minute walk ahead of him, weighed down by what was an obviously heavy burden, one which no one had yet questioned, much less examined, at any of the checkpoints he had passed through. Better to avoid them altogether than risk discovery by some jumpy or overzealous trigger-happy militiaman.

This time of year, the weather here always seemed milder than at home, some distance to the south. The intermittent gusts with occasional snow showers off the sea did little to wash away the noxious smell of the engine exhaust of idling tank and support vehicles. At virtually every major intersection, there was a conspicuous armed military presence supported by an armored personnel carrier or other Soviet-built hardware. They were stationed strategically throughout the city, ready to act instantly and violently on the slightest provocation or perceived opportunity. Illumination was in short supply on the streets except for occasional street lamps or the headlights of the military vehicles reflecting off the few puddles in the streets or windows with shades tightly drawn. It was nearly 11:00 P.M., curfew was in force, and the streets showed no evidence of the coming Christmas holiday. Even with his burden he moved briskly but cautiously away from the main train station, keeping to the shadows and avoiding any patches of light. He turned south and moved along Stolarski Street toward the Old Town until he reached a group of three-story apartment buildings a hundred meters from a hulking Nazi-era concrete bunker. He hurried into the yard between two of the structures and disappeared into a building entrance.

———

The suffocating police and military presence was unusual even for Peoples' Poland, but a military coup imposing martial law had been announced just two days earlier on Sunday at 6:00 A.M. in a special television address by General Wojciech Jaruzelski, since February the Prime Minister of Poland, but now the self-proclaimed military dictator. Throughout the whole year, there had been increasing unrest in Poland as the Solidarity Movement led by Lech Wałęsa spread and strengthened. Wałęsa and his followers steadfastly refused to be co-opted into the increasingly discredited communist government, and after a summer of hunger demonstrations that threatened the collapse of the state, on December 13, 1981, Jaruzelski declared martial law in Poland, "to defend socialism". Arrests had already begun before midnight, hours in advance of his announcement. Curfews were quickly established, national borders were sealed, military vehicles and squads of paramilitary riot police were assigned to patrol the streets of the major cities, and access to all cities by non-residents was sharply curtailed. Those limitations made it difficult for citizens in the metropolitan areas to obtain food, since rural residents became reluctant to surrender their products to the government at artificially low prices, and independent travel to the larger markets by individual farmers became difficult, if not impossible. Stricter rationing was imposed, even of the most basic foodstuffs, yet store shelves were empty, as they had been for months. Schools and universities were closed, and protests were met with savage, often fatal, repression. Squads of police brandishing riot shields like demounted medieval knights became a common but no less frightening sight on the urban streets of Poland.

With winter approaching, this far north the evenings came early. The wind off the Baltic rattled windows and nerves throughout Poland's fourth-largest city, and curfew was in force from 9:00 P.M. to 6:00 A.M. Czesław Kiedrowski and his family had lived in Gdańsk for many years. Together with their two teenagers, he and his wife Tamara now felt more like inmates than citizens, locked down in their own city. Christmas was just ten days away, but as was the case with most Poles now, the joyous holiday mood was conspicuously absent from their household. Soldiers were everywhere, and military vehicles rumbled through the streets, a vivid reminder to everyone of the military control of all aspects of Polish life. Workers in critical industries who didn't follow military orders imposed at work were threatened with court-martial. Movement by pedestrians within the cities was severely restricted. In fact, all civilian mobility was drastically limited throughout Poland, and Gdańsk, with its Lenin Shipyard cradle of Solidarity, the hotbed of opposition, was singled out among all Polish cities for special control. The workers of Gdańsk, a city with a thousand-year history as Danzig, a vital economic hub between eastern and western Europe, now became the drivers of a political movement that would ultimately transform not only Poland but Europe as well by the end of the decade.

On that cold, damp December night, there was a knock at

the door of Czesław and Tamara's third-floor apartment. Across Poland, for the past three nights, unexpected visits announced by more forceful knocks at the door for less than the celebratory purposes of the holiday season had been taking place. Thousands suspected of being government opponents or members of Solidarity were being rousted from their homes and arrested in front of their friends and families, and imprisoned. Some would not be released for more than five years. It was a crackdown on civilian dissidents to an extent that had been unknown in the decades since the vicious early months of the Nazi occupation, a time never far from Czesław's memory, when his parents were arrested and sent to labor camps, and he was sent to live with relatives. Even a tentative, conspiratorial knock late at night was troubling, and when Czesław finally approached the door and cautiously asked, "who's there?" the answer came back "Zbyszek." He flung open the door without hesitation.

At the door stood Czesław's younger brother, with a bulging backpack full of sausages and ham from a state-owned pig illegally butchered by his mother-in-law for this occasion. Zbigniew and his family lived in Złotów, more than 75 km away. He had traveled by train on a purely fabricated emergency trip to a gravely ill family member (Czesław) who, in fact, was in perfect health. He had wound his way through and around the intense police and military activity to ensure that his brother and family would have sufficient food to celebrate the holidays in appropriate fashion in spite of rationing and shortages.

Because telephone communication in Poland had been problematic for weeks, there was no way for the authorities to check on his story, but neither was there any way to contact Czesław and Tamara to let them know of his trip because they had no telephone. Nevertheless, in Gdańsk, it was especially crucial to avoid the police patrols where possible lest anyone local be able to investigate the story and find him out. He had left his home on that December afternoon of 1981, traveling that distance, changing trains twice, carrying provisions for his brother and family. There was little more important than reaching out to his brother and family in this time of crisis during the holiday season. At substantial physical risk, he lugged contraband food through the darkness and December weather, dodging soldiers and police to help his brother.

Across Poland that Tuesday night just two days after the coup, discussions in families like theirs naturally ran less to the coming holiday than to the grim reality of politics and society in the Peoples' Republic of Poland. Conversations touched on the bleak future for young people growing up in a country isolated from the West, where foreign language study was largely limited to Russian, private initiative was stifled, industry and commerce were stunted, and an economy of perpetual dearth squeezed the population ever harder in this colony of the Soviet Union. Even the controversial role of the Catholic Church in communist Poland could not escape their discussion, no less spirited a controversy since 1978 with a Polish Pope in Rome. With the exception of the inter-war years of the twentieth century, since the Partitions of Poland in 1772, the Catholic Church had been virtually the sole surviving custodian of Polish culture through partition, occupation and oppression, and it did so by largely remaining above politics. But a tenuous truce in its historically contentious relationship with the communist government had started to unravel, and the message from the pulpits of Poland was slowly taking on ominous, even dangerous tones. Not every parishioner found that trend acceptable, and many of those that didn't joined less political parishes, while others found the new message hopeful. Both positions found advocates in this family, adding yet another subject for their discussions.

As adults, the brothers had known nothing but communism as the political and social system dominating their lives, even though until in their teens they had experienced both the Second Polish Republic in its 1930s decline into military authoritarianism, and the savagery of the subsequent German invasion and Nazi occupation. Having been forcefully separated from each other and their parents for years, the stability and predictability provided by communism since 1947 was almost welcome, but that evening change was in that raw wind off the Baltic.

The discussions that evening were similar to what their father and uncles had likely engaged in decades earlier in similar circumstances under different regimes in familiar locales. But that shared secret from more than thirty years ago, when an uncle they had never met offered to bring Czesław to America, threatening to separate the family again, that created a rift between their parents and had never been forgotten. That incident, rarely discussed but never far in the back of their minds, could stir feelings again in times of crisis like this. It would re-energize the tradition of commitment to family that trumped politics, distance and even law for the brothers, a trait that often jeopardized personal safety and even life itself, as it did again that night of building oppression.

The two uncles who lived abroad through their efforts during and after World War II had achieved near-mythic stature in the eyes of their Polish brothers, sister, nieces and nephews. The stories passed down from parents to children were heroic tributes to uncles they had never known. Johann, reputed to have Heinrich Himmler as a friend, was instrumental in lessening or ending the labor camp terms of Władysław and Klara. In reality, at the very least, his hiring of a genealogist to prove German, not Polish, roots may have played a role. Sigmund had sent money and food to family as soon as possible and had offered to foster Czesław after the war. Nearly two decades after the last of the uncles had died, the legacy of fraternal commitment was no less apparent in this crisis for these two brothers in 1981 than it had been in the past for their father and his brothers and sister, especially during periods when they felt like unwilling immigrants in their own homeland occupied by alien regimes of oppression.

Though separated by oceans and armies, those ordinary people were unable to avoid the same political and social ideologies that disrupted and terminated the lives of millions like them, virulent ideologies that in their lifetimes created the entire spectrum of human experience from the bright promise of democratic self-determination to the unyielding gloom of communism. With unfeeling ferocity, life had sought out those siblings where they lived, enveloped them in a crushing embrace or alternatively swept them away dismissively across countries and continents from the small ethnic community where they were born. Those family members endured the fate of migrants, that defining figure of the twentieth century and one that would enflame political passions in the twenty-first. They all suffered through the same disruptions migrants experience, but not all crossed borders. Just two left their homeland intentionally and with purpose, but all experienced the triple losses of place, language and social code that the usual migrant encounters. More than once, borders were moved to enclose them in a different state and impose on them contrary values and unfamiliar language in the land of their birth.

Though some were casualties of the unspeakable horrors of this most brutal century in human history, those who survived – whether in Poland, Germany or America – proved closer to each other than distance or events seemed to allow. For those who had become immigrants in their own homeland, after enduring seemingly endless decades of chaos, conflict and repression, now once again the family bond between brothers was being tested. They were on the cusp of a change that would shock the world a decade later. It was not unlike what had shaken the world in 1918 with the collapse of empires and the creation of new nation-states in the aftermath of World War I. The promise of that time was erased twenty-one years later in an even more horrendous conflict on an even broader scale. In these dark days of December 1981, there was little indication of the coming change, but these brothers were no less devoted to each other than their uncles had been. Ironically, the two brothers who left that indelible mark on this next generation were the ones who had abandoned their ancestral roots. Their choice to claim German ancestry did not, however, deter them from reaching out to their family in Poland, as they proved during the war and the postwar period.

As young boys, Czesław and Zbigniew had been subjected to intense pressure by Nazi invaders to renounce their Polish cultural roots and embrace the German. But both had survived with roots intact and firmly planted. They displayed remarkable resilience in the face of repeated invasion, occupation, and assault on their native culture, first by Nazi, then by communist occupiers. Their lives were examples of what millions of people in central and eastern Europe experienced in the twentieth century. To family abroad, they were the secret vanguard and silent bearers of not only Polish ancestry, but Kashubian as well.

APPENDIX I
On the Family Name

Fixed family names did not appear in Poland until the fifteenth century, and then only by nobles, adopting the toponymic variety of surnames based on their estate or village name. In the case of the Kiedrowskis, the toponymic name that was used related to the village of Kiedrowice. The first written mention of the village that would become Kiedrowice is in a Latin document dated 1370, referring to "Kedrovo". References to Kiedrowice or the many variants of this name do not pre-date the fourteenth century. The origins of the name are the source for much discussion, ranging from "the place of the sons of Kieder", derived from the personal name Kieder, or even a corruption of Theodore.[41] It's unclear whether the origins are Polish or Germanic. If Germanic, it could be a modification of the ancient given name Godehar, or it could come from a word meaning "bait" or "trap". So, it could be that the village was where a trapper lived and pursued his livelihood.

Another explanation comes from a much more creative legend, that of the "Knight Leon von Kedros". According to this story, a young squire to a twelfth-century knight on the Third Crusade saved his sleeping lord from a lion who attacked the lord under a cedar tree – κέδρος in Greek. The squire was rewarded with a knighthood as "Leon of the Cedar" and was later given a land grant equivalent to about 16,000 acres. This story is much more entertaining than others proposed, but its origin as an oral tradition without convincing evidence over several hundred years makes it no more believable than other

---

[41] Noted Polish genealogist William "Fred" Hoffman, citing volume 4 of Kazimierz Rymut's *Nazwy miejscowe Polski* (Place Names of Poland), noted these possibilities in a personal email to the author March 3, 2006.

speculation.

But this family toponymic was complicated by the pre-existing clan names that had pre-dated family surnames. In Poland, a clan was not exclusive to one family. The same coat of arms (*herb* in Polish) could be legally approved for several different families. Different families were subsumed under one coat of arms. Eventually, this unusual system led to one clan made up of different families and, conversely, people with the same surname having different coats of arms. The Kiedrowskis in Kashubia used variants on their coats of arms as well, including Ostoja, Kojtala and Sas.[42]

In the case of the Kiedrowski family, the progenitors of Anton and Anna's children adopted the *Lew* (lion) coat of arms, which some authorities (Klaus Liwowsky) have considered an extended family of coats of arms. Occasionally in documents, the Lew was added later as a superscript after being omitted entirely. And to add even further to the confusion, there were non-noble families in the area with the surname Lew. Nowhere are nobles from the Kiedrowski family indicated simply as "the noble Lew", i.e., simply by their coat of arms. Most likely, the first Kiedrowski to use the coat of arms formally was Adalbert, born in the early seventeenth century. His son, Martin (1673-1768), definitely used the coat of arms as part of his now three-part name: Martin Lew Kiedrowski.

To complicate the name just a bit more, in Latin documents, the preposition *de* (from/of) was inserted between the Lew and the Kiedrowski, denoting nobility. In German documents during the occupation of the area by Prussia, later Germany, *von* was the prefix of choice and sometimes even preceded the Lew, which itself evolved into Loewe/Löwe. The somewhat tortuous evolution by the end of the nineteenth

---

[42] Przemysław Pragert, *Herbarz Szlachty Kaszubskiej*, (Gdańsk, BiT, 2007), Tom 2, pp. 88-89.

century was Kiedrowski → Lew Kiedrowski → Lew de Kiedrowski → Lew von Kiedrowski → von Lew Kiedrowski → von Löwe Kiedrowski. Further complicating matters is that in German, "von" could be used to indicate where someone is from – "Hans from Kiedrowice" could be misinterpreted by some to indicate nobility when in fact, it does not.

The German influence on some members of this family and its surname is clearly revealed in Johann's name change in 1931, which he caused to be noted on his civil birth certificate from 1881, as well as Sigmund's choice for becoming an American citizen.[43] Other members of this family in Germany today use variously von Löwe and von Kiedrowski, or just plain Kiedrowski. Löwe, with or without the von, and its many variations in Germany is widespread, and usually not associated with this family with its Kashubian roots. It could be claimed that more "lions" roam Germany than Africa.

---

[43] There seems, however, to be no evidence that any of Sas, Ostoja or Kojtala Kiedrowskis changed their family name to Ostoja, etc.

APPENDIX II
The Diamond Cipher

As reported in Chapter Four, "Pivot", Sigmund used enciphered and encoded entries to describe in a pocket calendar for 1925 his 1920 play in the diamond market. Typical for the time, each page in the calendar section comprises four days, each separated from the others by a horizontal red line. Within each day portion, there are five lines for entering events or notations. Sigmund made only a few entries in those pages, some of which are inspirational quotes in German, and on one date – Christmas Day – is noted the death of "v. Bismarck" in 1898. Otto von Bismarck died on July 30, 1898, so the calendar was less a calendar and more a notebook for important events or thoughts.

It is the final page of the calendar year, December 31, which reveals the notes describing the progress and chronology of the diamond deal. On the four-section page, there is only that day at the top. There are five entries on that page, two in cleartext, more or less easily readable in German, English or Polish, and three in German ciphertext.

The top section lists diamonds; Sigmund wrote "DiAM." to the right of the list, vertically from bottom to top. The first column in the list indicates the number of stones, the second column most likely color. There are three types noted, "SiLVA", SILBER", and "S.NEGER". The third column indicates carat weight, e.g., 0.35, etc. The "silber" stones, of which there were twelve, are indicated as "X" in the weight column, most likely indicating 1/10 of a carat, as is the one "s.neger" stone. In all, there are twenty-one diamonds ranging in size from .1 to .75 carat. This list comprised nearly four carats of diamonds.[44] Below this list is written in mixed German/English cleartext "LETZTE 3 WEEKS VOR OSTERN 1921", (Last three weeks before Easter 1921) with a line below this sentence to separate it from the next entry on the page. Interesting is that he used the English word for weeks, not the German *Wochen*. Easter that year fell on March 27, so he was referring to the period March 6-27, 1921.

Sigmund recorded this inventory of loose diamonds in this calendar probably no earlier than September 1924 as he recalled it and related events from more than three years earlier. This was either a feat of remarkable memory or a copying of notes he carried with him together with stones in folded diamond paper that he had retained from before he came to America. Heavy tissue paper-like diamond paper, with its multiple crisp folds to keep the diamonds secure, is easily concealed in a shirt pocket or passport case, and contents could have been noted on an

---

[44] In general, larger stones have a greater value per carat than smaller ones of the same quality. It is tempting to try to assign a value to these stones, adjusted for inflation, but nowadays there are so many factors involved even beyond cut, color and clarity, that it would be difficult to determine from the limited descriptions. Suffice it to say that the inventory probably had more real value in America than in either Germany or Poland. The use of the term "neger" could have indicated these stones were black, not the usual white/blue diamond.

inside fold of the paper. Diamonds' portability and extraordinarily high value-to-weight ratio make them a substitute currency during economic troubles such as Poland and Germany were experiencing in 1921. Bringing them into an economy with a more stable currency as America had in 1923 could be very profitable. Those stones acquired in 1921 were still in memory in great detail or in hand in 1924. He was not known for keeping sloppy records in business, least of all with gemstones. The next entry on the page for December 31, 1925, offers a clue, though heavily encrypted and encoded.

Section 2 on that page consists of three lines of ciphertext:

BUBLOLUTOT-ABUBNONAHACHM.

4.4.21.

APRIL 11. 1921 NONEGOGTOT.

This seems to be a simple transposition cipher written in German. Consonant-vowel-consonant combinations were used as infixes in the words to confuse the reader (even German-speaking ones), although there were a couple of instances of consonant-vowel-consonant-consonant. The final consonant in a repetitive combination was the one preserved, followed by letters not in that group.

Deciphered:

BLUT-ABNAHM

4.4.21.

APRIL 11. 1921 NEGT.

The translation from German seems to be:

Blood Loss

4.4.21.

April 11, 1921 Negative

This entry follows on the page and chronologically the inventory of diamonds, but suggests a blood loss test that proved negative. How was that connected to the diamonds? The next entry also seems unrelated to the diamonds. Enciphered, it reads:

ANONGUGESISTOTECKTX
UM MITTE OCKTOBER 1920

He mixed the cipher with the second line in German cleartext, though misspelling the month of October, probably confusing it with English.
Deciphered:

ANGESTECKTEN
UM MITTE OCKTOBER 1920

A translation from German yields:

Infected
Around the middle of October 1920

During October 1920, he was still employed by Klüppelholz. If this was a health issue, why record it four years later, and in cipher?
The fourth entry follows chronologically the third, enciphered:

BUBEHOUHANONDODLOLUNONGUGIXE.
ANONFOCHANONGOG
CIRCA 10. NONOV. '20

Deciphered it reads:

BEHANDLUNG
ANFOCHANG
CIRCA 10. NOV. '20

The deciphering of the second line leading to the word *anfochang* suggests Sigmund's fingers slipped while writing in manuscript, or he lost his place in the enciphering process. The infix "OCH" seems to be an error, and the word would be more likely rendered as "Anfang", or beginning. Translated from the German:

Treatment
Beginning
Around 10 November 1920

The final entry on this page is cleartext Polish:

Boże pomocz mnie

Translated from Sigmund's Polish: God help me.

Arranging everything on this page in chronological order, we learn that Sigmund was "infected" about the middle of October 1920, while he still worked for Klüppelholz, and began "treatment" around November 10, after he had left that job. Four months later, in late March 1921,[45] he was in possession of several carats of diamonds and, on April 4 of that year, eight days after Easter, had a blood test that a week later proved "negative".

A health issue seems out of place in such close association with a list of loose diamonds. In fact, it seems that the enciphered entries are just the beginning of Sigmund's attempt to confound an unintended reader of his calendar. In

---

[45] The new constitution for Poland was signed March 17, 1921.

all likelihood, those entries are code phrases for business dealings the young watchmaker and jeweler entered into or at least attempted to. There would be little reason to encipher medical problems but a good reason to encipher business transactions, especially if they were particularly memorable, compromising – or sketchy.

There is a distinct possibility that the cipher was used to further obscure code phrases, offering even further protection from prying eyes. For example, take the cleartext:

CLIMB MT NIITAKA

This phrase could be enciphered using the basic Caesar cipher shift of three:[46]

FOLPEPWQLLWDND

Even deciphering might not give a meaningful answer if the message is a military one, and is code for "Climb Mt. Niitaka" (the Japanese Navy command to attack Pearl Harbor as planned). Just as the "climb Mt Niitaka" was an agreed-upon code phrase to indicate a planned military attack was to be executed, so could "infected in the middle of October" have some special meaning to Sigmund in terms of a business opportunity.

In anticipation of being unemployed by the end of the month and encountering a business opportunity that appeared attractive enough for him to become involved in, he started negotiating for the stones while still working for Klüppelholz. It may even be that he was paid by Klüppelholz in diamonds and sought to liquidate them into local currency.

---

[46] A letter is enciphered by the letter three places down in the alphabet, e.g. A is enciphered as D, B as E, etc.

In any case, according to the notes, he initiated discussions on this business matter involving diamonds ten days after he left the job,[47] completing an agreement four months later, in late March 1921. This new undertaking may have resulted in the acquisition of a number of diamonds, but this enterprise related to the gemstones did not take the course he expected, resulting in that negative result. The diamonds are central to this period of time, and the events described in April suggest an unsuccessful outcome. The listing of the stones in such detail three years later suggests that he brought them with him to America, where their expected increase in value over wartime lows could be useful to a new immigrant, either as currency or as raw material for his own jewelry-making enterprise. To record such a specific table three years after the fact is a remarkable feat of memory – or they were still in his possession.

His cipher is used in one other entry in the calendar, under November 19, a "birthday" (written in cleartext English):

ESISTOTEROR SISCHACHULDZAUN

which, using the same system of cipher, seems to yield:

ESTER SCHULDZAUN

This is just one more mystery. Was "Ester" somehow related to the diamond transaction as an agent for the cutter, other provider or prospective purchaser? The encryption of this personal surname is especially peculiar since the un-enciphered surname is non-existent in Germany (or Poland)

---

[47] Maybe not so coincidentally the Free City of Danzig became an official entity on November 9, 1920, perhaps opening up the opportunities for Sigmund in the diamond trade. The next day is when "treatment began". He was in Danzig on May 7, and also from December 22 to 30.

today. This could also be Schun or Schulz, family names found in Germany today, but Sigmund's apparent "rules" would have been slightly modified to give these results. To encrypt the name in German, but the event in clear English seems unusual, but is not atypical for Sigmund's cipher as noted above. Or was the name just another code? Since it seems to be the same cipher as the diamond page, it is likely related to the transaction, with a role unclear. The name does not occur anywhere else in the calendar, but part of a page in the address section has been carefully torn out and may have contained information about her. Just another puzzle created by Sigmund.

BIBLIOGRAPHY

The following works are representative of specific areas I cover in this work but are an infinitesimally small subset of the literature on twentieth-century European history.

Borzyszkowski, Józef, *The Kashubs, Pomerania and Gdańsk*. Translated by Tomasz Wicherkiewicz. Gdańsk: Kashubian Institute in Gdańsk, 2005.

Cienciala, Anna, Natalia S. Lebedeva, and Wojciech Materski, editors. *Katyn: A Crime Without Punishment*. New Haven, CT: Yale University Press, 2007.

Cooke, David C., *Sky Battle: 1914-1918: The Story of Aviation in World War I*. New York: W.W. Norton, 1970.

Davies, Norman, *God's Playground: A History of Poland*. 2 vols. New York: Columbia University Press, 2005.

de Zayas, Alfred-Maurice. *A Terrible Revenge: The Ethnic Cleansing of the East European Germans*. New York: Palgrave Macmillan, 2006.

Douglas, R.M., *Orderly and Humane: The Expulsion of the Germans after the Second World War*. New Haven, CT: Yale University Press, 2012.

Duiven, Rick and Dan-San Abbott. *Schlacht-Flieger!* Atglen, Pennsylvana: Schiffer Military History, 2006.

Franks, Norman, Frank Bailey and Rick Duiven. *The Jasta Pilots: Detailed Listings and Histories, August 1916 – November 1918*. London: Grub Street, 1996.

Fritzsche, Peter, *A Nation of Fliers: German Aviation and the Popular Imagination*. Cambridge, MA: Harvard University Press, 1992.

Fritzsche, Peter, *An Iron Wind: Europe Under Hitler* New York: Basic Books, 2016.

Frymark, Stanisłôw, *Kashubian Language in Canada, the USA and New Zealand.* Zaborsk, Poland: Zómk Zôbórsczi, 2020.

Gerwarth, Robert. *The Vanquished: Why the First World War Failed to End.* New York: Farrar, Straus, and Giroux, 2016.

Helm, Sarah. *Ravensbrück: Life and Death in Hitler's Concentration Camp for Women.* New York: Anchor Books, 2016.

Kennett, Lee. *The First Air War: 1914-1918.* New York: Simon & Schuster, 1999.

Lowe, Keith. *Savage Continent: Europe in the Aftermath of World War II.* New York: St. Martin's Press, 2012.

Lukas, Richard C. *The Forgotten Holocaust: The Poles under German Occupation 1939-1944.* New York: Hippocrene Books, 1990.

Macmillan, Margaret. *Paris 1919: Six Months that Changed the World.* New York: Random House, 2001.

Macintyre, Ben. *Agent Sonya: Moscow's Most Daring Wartime Spy.* New York: Penguin Random House, 2020.

Millet, Larry. *Lost Twin Cities.* St. Paul, MN: Minnesota Historical Society Press, 1992.

Millet, Larry. *Metropolitan Dreams: The Scandalous Rise and Stunning Fall of a Minneapolis Masterpiece.* Minneapolis: University of Minnesota Press, 2018.

Moorhouse, Roger. *First to Fight: The Polish War 1939.* London: Vintage, 2020.

Morsch, Günter and Astrid Ley (ed.). *Sachsenhausen*

Concentration Camp: 1936-1945 Events and Developments. Berlin: Metropol Verlag, 2011.

Obracht-Prondzyński and Tomasz Wicherkiewiec, eds. *The Kashubs: Past and Present.* Bern, Switzerland: Peter Lang, AG, 2011.

Okrent, Daniel. *The Guarded Gate: Bigotry, Eugenics, and the Law That Kept Two Generations of Jews, Italians, and Other European Immigrants Out of America.* New York: Scribner, 2019.

Olson, Lynne. *Last Hope Island: Britain, Occupied Europe, and the Brotherhood That Helped Turn the Tide of War.* New York: Random House, 2017.

Pragert, Przemysław. *Herbarz Szlachty Kaszubskiej* [Armorial of Kashubian Nobility]. 2 vols. Gdańsk: BiT, 2007.

Rekowski, Aloysius J. *The Saga of the Kashub People in Poland, Canada, U.S.A.* Saskatoon, Canada: A.J. Rekowski, 1997.

Rushdie, Salman. "On Günter Grass", *Granta,* March 1985.

Schilling, Franz, and Helmut Rettinghaus. *Die Geschichte der Luftpolizei* [The History of the Air Police]. Illertissen, Germany: Flugzeug Publikations GmbH, 1994.

Shulist, David Martin. *Discovering Kashubia Europe, The Fatherland of my Kashubian ancestors.* Ottawa, Canada: Gilmore Doculink & David Martin Shulist, 2018.

Snyder, Timothy. *Bloodlands: Europe Between Hitler and Stalin.* New York: Basic Books, 2012.

VanWyngarden, G., *Early German Aces of World War I.* Oxford, England: Osprey Publishing, 2006.

Wilkins, Mark, "The Dark Side of Glory; an Early Glimpse of PTSD in the Letters of World War I Aces," *Air & Space Smithsonian,* March 2018, pp. 54-59.

INTERNET LINKS

Keller, R.H., "The German Soldier in World War I; the Final 'Argument of Kings'," (2009), accessed October 15, 2020, https://greatwar.com/the-german-soldier/.

Sherman, Stephen, "Ernst Udet – Second Highest German Ace of World War I," accessed October 15, 2020, http://www.acepilots.com/wwi/ger_udet.html.

http://www.gazetakaszubska.pl/ [The Kashubian Newspaper]

ACKNOWLEDGEMENTS

The general story of my research for this book was told in the Prologue. Many of the most helpful people were mentioned there, but some remain unidentified. Not the least of them are the good people who volunteered at the Family History Center of the East Brunswick Church of the Latter-Day Saints. The many Saturday mornings I spent with them in the course of my research were made easier because of their efforts.

The crucial breakthrough to family in Poland came about through the efforts of Wanda and Franciszek Lew Kiedrowski, who since 2001 have hosted the family reunion at their conference center and agro-tourism inn in Pażęce. It was Wanda, a leader in the Kashubian community, who reached out to Czesław and told him of my inquiry into the family gathering. And, of course, Czesław's daughter Katrina was key to my learning of my aunt, uncles, and their families. Without her as translator and intermediary, much of what I learned of the family would simply not exist. Among the many photos she shared with me, she provided the photos of Anton's pocket watch used here. She was extraordinarily giving of her time and knowledge, and I will always be in her debt.

Two other individuals in Poland, but not closely related to me, provided much information and insight into the family. Zbigniew Kiedrowski of Człuchów wrote a remarkably thorough history of the Lew Kiedrowskis and shared everything generously with me. On the basis of documents he easily disproved some of the more questionable assertions put forth by some other family members outside of Poland. He and his wife Bożena provided extraordinary hospitality to our 2008 visiting family crew of six. Stanley Frymark, Kashubian partisan, linguist and inn-keeper of Zamek Zaborski, since 2004 has been my go-to guy for documents that were photographed and copied to CDs and other media. He is also my reliable interpreter of Kashubian culture.

Prominent in my personal pantheon of Polish family heroes is Ryszard Felski. He is the grandson of my uncle Anastazy, the national police officer murdered at Katyń, and son of Anastazy's daughter Maria. Maria kept albums of photos, and Ryszard shared them all with me. Remarkably, almost all of the photos were correctly identified. Among them used here are the photo of August Kiedrowski in 1918 and the 1923 studio photo of Władysław, Klemens, Sigmund, and Anastazy. She also kept the letter Sigmund sent her when she sought assistance after the war, and Ryszard shared it with me. Judy and I visited them in Tuchola, where Ryszard and his wife Krystyna opened their house and family to us for several days in 2013, showing a breath-taking level of hospitality unusual even for Poland.

In Germany, Uwe Kiedrowski of Dortmund has compiled a list of Kiedrowskis around the world. It is a useful collection, simply by magnitude of numbers, but is unpublished, copyrighted in 2006. As a participant in several online genealogy communities, I was fortunate to have a lot of assistance in my research from members. Traute Buck was extraordinarily helpful in transcribing an otherwise unreadable letter between the two brothers Heinz and Hans von Loewe. Heinz Radde was an incredible sounding board on name changes in Germany. William F. "Fred" Hoffman was always responsive to my questions about the family name. Debbie Greenlee gave me a broader perspective on Poland in general in her job as moderator of the Polish Genius online community.

Closer to home, two former colleagues and dear friends from my years in the history department at Rutgers University deserve recognition here. Michael Adas and his wife, Jane, have been supportive of this project from its inception and have offered many useful remarks. David R. Ringrose parsed out an earlier manuscript and provided comments that substantially improved it; I leave it to the reader's imagination what it would have been without Dave's efforts.

Ray von Loewe, son of Hans, grandson of Johann, and his wife, Barb, are indefatigable travelers, and we tested them in 2008. Their good cheer and cooperative spirit contributed to that trip. Ray provided me with the letters from family in Germany to his father from 1937 to 1978, a treasure of family memories. The letters made personal for me the postwar troubles they faced.

My wife, Judy, has been an unflagging source of support, encouragement and tolerance through all the years of my research and writing, notwithstanding her rarely-voiced (and not unreasonable) preference that my research interest would have been the French Riviera.

ABOUT THE AUTHOR

Karl von Loewe is a graduate of Macalester College and earned a master's degree in Slavic languages and literatures and a Ph.D. in history from the University of Kansas. He has lived and traveled widely in Russia and eastern Europe as a graduate student, researcher and genealogist. The author of several scholarly publications, his extensive academic research, residence and travel helped provide context for the family story in *Lost Roots*.

He and his infinitely patient wife reside in New Jersey, where they share staff duties for a mouthy cat.

ABOUT ATMOSPHERE PRESS

Atmosphere Press is an independent, full-service publisher for excellent books in all genres and for all audiences. Learn more about what we do at atmospherepress.com.

We encourage you to check out some of Atmosphere's latest releases, which are available at Amazon.com and via order from your local bookstore:

The Swing: A Muse's Memoir About Keeping the Artist Alive, by Susan Dennis

Possibilities with Parkinson's: A Fresh Look, by Dr. C

Gaining Altitude - Retirement and Beyond, by Rebecca Milliken

Out and Back: Essays on a Family in Motion, by Elizabeth Templeman

Just Be Honest, by Cindy Yates

You Crazy Vegan: Coming Out as a Vegan Intuitive, by Jessica Ang

Detour: Lose Your Way, Find Your Path, by S. Mariah Rose

To B&B or Not to B&B: Deromanticizing the Dream, by Sue Marko

Convergence: The Interconnection of Extraordinary Experiences, by Barbara Mango and Lynn Miller

Sacred Fool, by Nathan Dean Talamantez

My Place in the Spiral, by Rebecca Beardsall

My Eight Dads, by Mark Kirby

Dinner's Ready! Recipes for Working Moms, by Rebecca Cailor

Vespers' Lament: Essays Culture Critique, Future Suffering, and Christian Salvation, by Brian Howard Luce

Without Her: Memoir of a Family, by Patsy Creedy

CPSIA information can be obtained
at www.ICGtesting.com
Printed in the USA
JSHW050933270522
26427JS00001B/4